Dispatches from a Borderless World

Dispatches from a Borderless World

Satya Das

NeWest Press
Edmonton

Canadian Cataloguing in Publication Data
Das, Satya, 1955-
  Dispatches from a borderless world

ISBN 1-896300-42-1

  1. International economic integration. 2. Ethnocentrism.
3. Canadians. I. Title.
JC362.D37 1999   337   C99-910240-0

Editor for the Press: Don Kerr
Cover design: John Luckhurst/GDL
Interior design: Brenda Burgess
Cover photographs: Satya Das

NeWest Press acknowledges the support of the Canada Council for the Arts for our publishing program. We also acknowledge the financial support of the Government of Canada through the Book Publishing Industry Development Program (BPIDP) for our publishing activities and the Department of Canadian Heritage.

Canadian Heritage   Patrimoine canadien   Canada

Photographs have been reproduced with the kind permission of the author and John Luckhurst.

Seferis, George; *George Seferis Collected Poems*, translated by Edmund Keeley and Philip Sherrard. Copyright © 1967 by Princeton University Press. Reprinted by permission of Princeton University Press.

All material except the original pieces "Becoming Canadian in England" and "How the borderless world came to be born" reprinted by the kind permission of the *Edmonton Journal*.

Every effort has been made to obtain permission for quoted material. If there is an omission or error the author and publisher would be grateful to be so informed.

Printed and bound in Canada

NeWest Publishers Limited
Suite 201, 8540–109 Street
Edmonton, Alberta T6G 1E6

To the memory of my ancestors

And to my family:

Grandmother Nilamani

Parents Gita and Jagannath

Parents-in-law Urmila and Prafulla

Daughters Silpi and Somya

Sister Sheela

And my beloved wife and companion, Mita,

who makes all things possible

Δε θελω τιποτε αλλο παρα να μιλησω απλα,
να που δοθει ετουτι η χαρι.

—ΣΕΦΕΡΙΣ

I want no more than to speak simply, to be granted that grace.

—*SEFERIS*

Table of Contents

Acknowledgements

Many of the works in *Dispatches from a Borderless World* first appeared in the *Edmonton Journal*, where I began working in 1977. My first thanks go to Duart Farquharson, Linda Goyette, and Allan Chambers, who offered me the benefit of their ideas, intellects, and companionship during our stimulating years together on an exceptionally lively and collegial editorial board.

My writing would not have been possible without the interest of my mentors: Barry Westgate, Linda Hughes, and Donald Romaniuk offered invaluable encouragement during my formative years in journalism; Rudy Wiebe and the late Marian Engel gave me a writer's freedom to imagine.

I am also grateful to Murdoch Davis, the *Journal*'s current editor-in-chief, for permitting publication of essays whose copyright the *Journal* holds, and for financing the travel involved in many of these Dispatches. Peter Richards and Ron Richardson of the Asia Pacific Foundation of Canada often pointed me in the right direction.

My notions of the Borderless World began to take shape in the Thatcher era in Britain. My thanks to the Nuffield Foundation for taking me there on a fellowship at Wolfson College Cambridge in 1987, and to Bill Kirkman and Sir David Williams for welcoming me with a warmth and generosity I cannot hope to repay.

My special thanks to the poet Don Kerr, whose sensitive editing of the manuscript brought many useful changes; and to Liz Grieve, Kathy Chiles, and Jennifer Bellward at NeWest Press for their kindness and assistance. The errors and faults readers will find are entirely my own.

Satya Das
Edmonton

Acknowledgments

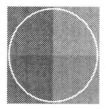

To Begin

Less than five years ago, Sarala graduated from an engineering college in Orissa, the rustic eastern Indian state where I was born. Since he was trained in computers, he hoped for a good career, but he really didn't expect what came next.

Only months into his first job in the Indian capital New Delhi, he was hired away by France's largest telecommunications company. Speaking no French, he found himself living in a company apartment in the heart of Paris—a quick immersion into an often delightful culture that's as different as can be imagined from his native milieu. After hitting his stride in France, he took another leap across the world: landing a job with Saville Systems, the Irish-based multinational that has its roots, and a major presence, in Edmonton.

Sarala arrived in Edmonton last March and had yet to face his first Canadian winter. "You just have to dress for it," I told him when we met last fall. What else can you say to prepare someone for his or her baptism of ice? By midwinter, he had been offered an even better job in the United States.

His story is an increasingly common one in today's borderless world. The global economy, the flow of commerce and capital from one market to another, brings with it startling changes in the lives and circumstances of people with new skills.

Indian computer engineers are a hot commodity in the business world—the forty thousand who graduate each year are quickly snapped up, and there's always a demand for more.

As capital, commerce, and investment flow across borders, they carry people and cultures in their wake. And while there may be a profound understanding of the international flow of goods and services, there's far less understanding of cultural mingling. Unregulated markets and anarchic flows of capital are part of the reason the global recession of 1998 nearly became the undoing of capitalist economies, yet much of the difficulty arose from a fatal ignorance of how other societies work.

What happens when attitudes and assumptions formed in strikingly different cultural and historical contexts come face to face? This is the fascinating, evolving, and largely unexplored aspect of the borderless world. And it was insufficiently explored before the crash of 1998.

The currency speculators who move two trillion dollars around every day, affecting the standard of living in just about every country in the world, often have little knowledge of how their targeted countries really function. They look at numbers and bottom lines, and make decisions that can plunge even a stable country like Malaysia into turmoil.

When the march of global economics ignores the complex and essential task of understanding something of how countries, cultures, and societies work, chaos is bound to result. That's certainly the case with some of the economic shocks the world saw in 1998.

There are two striking examples: the general incomprehension in the West of the history and attitudes that shape Japan, the world's second most powerful economy; and nuclear-armed Russia's backward march from gangster capitalism to the uncertain charms of its communist past.

The great failure in Russia was the lazy assumption that free-market economics could quickly and easily take hold in a society emerging from a centrally planned command economy singularly lacking in original thought, critical reasoning, and constructive dissent. No one stopped long enough to consider the individualism required in the free-market is not enough: the success of market-oriented western democracies also arises out of a sense of social responsibility and obligation which is born and bred in a democracy.

In the absence of democracy, of the tradition and experience of living in and nurturing democratic institutions, capitalism becomes essentially anarchic: a survival-of-the-fittest that leaves the great majority of people cold and hungry in the snow. One can hardly blame ordinary Russians who yearn for the past, with all its patent shortcomings. The tragedy is no one in the West was wise enough to help Russia evolve towards the middle ground.

In the same vein, too little attention is paid to the communal and collectivist traditions of Japanese culture and history, which continue to shape the attitudes and character of modern Japan. It is the remarkable degree of social cohesion in a homogenous society—as opposed to the absence of tradition and the triumph of individualism in immigration-enriched countries like Canada and the United States—that really sets Japan apart.

It's futile to expect Japan will abandon its common-good approach to social and economic policy, and replace it with stridently individualistic practices. It would be equally silly to think the United States would even try to moderate its individual-first society with anything approaching the Canadian balance, by embracing government-funded health care or similar social programs.

Expecting one culture to behave by the patterns and traditions that are familiar to another is foolish and even arrogant. So far, it seems to be a defining flaw in the age of the global economy and the borderless world. The country that's best positioned to address the flaw is ours. Canada's unique strength, the ability to accommodate many streams of culture and human experience within a dynamic and evolving national identity, will gain more importance as the world becomes interlinked.

To prevent a recurrence of the 1998–99 global economic crisis and similar future shocks, it is all the more necessary to become fluent in the cultures of others. Just as languages were learned in an earlier age, so must cultures be learned in our time, if the intimacy bred by the communications revolution is to bring more good than harm. The singular advantage of Canada as an incubator and social laboratory of cultural mingling should not be underestimated. We may find, to our surprise, that the twentyfirst century does indeed belong to Canada, at least in offering a model of how the world might live together.

At one time, the Canadian perspective might not have seemed so important. Throughout the 1990s, questions of cultural and social harmony, a peaceful meeting of many streams of identity, seemed irrelevant in the march of global capitalism. The triumph of money, it was thought, would solve all. Economic forces would be the great emancipators, the great equalizer: the only culture to triumph would be the Cult of the Consumer, celebrated across the globe.

The anticipated triumph of a world made borderless by economics has yet to materialize, and it may never come about in the form trumpeted by the champions of free-flowing capital. By the summer of 1997, the first shock of what came to be known as the "Asian contagion" began to be felt. It took the worldwide spread of this economic virus to put a stop to the triumph of capital.

In late 1998, the most ardent champions of capital admitted as much. They killed the Multilateral Agreement on Investment (MAI). It was a small item in many newspapers on an October day, fittingly placed beside the obituaries, and for all the fuss given to it during its life, you would think its death would have been anything but a quiet one.

Yet quiet it was. With expressions more of reluctance than regret, the world's richer industrial countries declared the MAI is dead. Once the bright hope of global capitalism, the instrument that would open all borders to the free flow of investment and capital, the best hope for global prosperity in the eyes of its Canadian champion Donald Johnston, was allowed to slip away.

France's defection sealed its fate. France only delivered the coup de grâce. Even before the official announcement, governments the world over began to have second thoughts. The frightening consequences of uncontrolled capitalism, so evident in the global economic crisis that is yet to be quelled, at last brought some realism to starry eyes filled with promises of limitless prosperity.

How much prosperity would there really be, France rightly wondered, if all jobs and investment flowed to the world's lowest-cost markets—and developed countries were left with armies of unemployed people who might never regain a comfortable middle-class life? The death of the MAI ends for now the theory that unhindered global capitalism is the best way to build prosperity. If it's not, what is? As the world looks for a way out of crisis, it is becoming clear that the experience of Asia in the months and years ahead might become the trailblazer for any new global economic direction.

In October 1998, at the depth of the global economic crisis, I was invited to participate in an extraordinary gathering of scholars, diplomats, and high officials from Europe, Asia, and North America, held in Calgary. There was lots of straight talk around the table. Under the Chatham House rule—one can use everything that's said, but attribute nothing—the roundtable offered a pervasive sense that the health of the global economy depends largely—if not entirely—on Japan's and Asia's ability to rediscover themselves.

Participants listened attentively and took notes as speaker after speaker uttered what might have been considered socialist heresy only six months earlier. Calls for the Japanese government control of banks met with wise nods, as did calls for big-ticket government spending to make work for those left jobless by the crisis. There was all sorts of bitterness about the International Monetary Fund's IMF bungling of Asia's crisis, expressed in cutting jokes about the IMF posing a greater destructive threat to Asia than India and Pakistan's nuclear missiles.

Phrases to make a Canadian cringe emerged: some Asians feel the "Anglo-Saxons" look down contemptuously on the "yellow races." The Australian racist Pauline Hanson and a remarkably insular U.S. Congress with little sympathy or understanding of Japan's position were cited as prime examples. And because the "Caucasians are so powerful," the "yellow races" feel deeply uncomfortable in criticizing the IMF, no matter how wrong and damaging its policies were.

To hear such talk from a senior figure in a leading Asian country sent a ripple of discomfort around the room, before the deft conclusion. The only western country that makes Asians feel truly comfortable, said the speaker, the only country that treats Asians with respect, is Canada. So we Canadians are particularly welcome in Asia, and we will be the preferred partners, now that Asian countries know who their friends are. Attacks on the IMF, calls for currency control, and bank nationalization seem so unfashionable that they might even cause an embarrassed pause at New Democratic Party caucus meetings these days. Yet there they were, emanating from the battlefield generals of the capitalist wars.

That wasn't all. After enjoying the fruits of crony capitalism and corruption for decades, these veterans declared corruption must end—the fruits of growth and wealth creation must be equitably distributed and western investors must demand transparency and clean government in return for rebuilding Asian economies.

Such talk would have been regarded as naive if not dangerous when the Asian tigers were registering remarkable surges of growth. While the boom lasted, capitalists were only too happy to cozy up to whatever dictator was in charge—decisions were made so quickly, and any repression or injustice was an internal matter entirely divorced from business and commerce.

Is the era of globalization over? No. But as it is reborn, it will feature more government control over economic forces, the integration of social and political issues with economic ones. Participants thought the Canadian gathering had a more serious understanding of Japan and Asia's problems than anything they've heard so far in the United States.

And it seems a very Canadian sense of proportion and balance will win the day, as governments harness the forces of capitalism to serve the common good. That's the optimistic scenario. There are, of course, gloomier ones.

There is one certainty: no matter how the borderless world evolves, Canada and the Canadian experience will be of immense value as countries, cultures, people, and economies come together. The Global Village Marshall McLuhan predicted is taking shape with a speed that is at times dazzling. The dispatches gathered here capture the transformation of many parts of the world, yet the catalyst for the change is always the same: the advent of the information age.

Still, there is a paradox. Even as communications, commerce, and the ease of travel create a borderless world, there is a strong resistance to this forced elimination of boundaries. The resistance is more social and cultural than economic. It is remarkable that the United States, the most ardent champion of the free flow of capital, should become more inward looking and insular as its economic practices erase borders. The obsession with President Bill Clinton's sexual misdeeds at a time of great foment in the world is one instance. So is the presence of a military so huge it makes the United States the world's police by default—and the absolute reluctance to put that military to use if it means the actual deployment of U.S. troops in harm's way.

There is, too, the resolute drive to maintain national boundaries, create new nation states, and define pieces of territory with a homogenous identity. The Irish question, the never-ending dispute between Israelis and Palestinians, the litany of peace made and broken, amount to a drawing of boundaries, both personal and collective. Even in our own country, people agitating for an independent Quebec want the twenty-first-century equivalent of a nineteenth-century European nation state. By drawing boundaries around a culture, they say, they will be better able to flourish in a world where the English language dominates business and communications. Establishing boundaries, individual and collective, may seem at first to contradict the notion of a borderless world. It is very much a part of the evolution. The arrival of the information age no longer permits the luxury of isolation. The Internet reaches most parts of the globe, the arrival of the Iridium satellite phone and pager network means no place on the globe is beyond the reach of communication.

At one extreme, nationalists draw borders as though they were fortress walls. At the other are people like Sarala, nomads of the information age. For the decades of the Cold War, the expansionist attitudes of the former Soviet Union were described as Communists trying to create One World. The implication was clear: this is a prelude to totalitarian domination. "One worlder" became a term that implied treason. How ironic, then, that the communications revolution permits capitalism and commerce to create the One World once so feared. It enables the free flow of goods and services and money, but so far it bars the free flow of people. This too is the ultimate boundary, in a world where boundaries and borders are in danger. Mobility rights apply to an affluent elite, in countries like Canada that sell immigration visas to "entrepreneurs," or a less formal right of residence granted to the wealthy who may travel where they please. The strongest barriers that exist, the most stringent walls, are designed to keep people out, but let trade and investment in.

This simultaneous dismantling of old barriers and the erection of new ones is one of the more fascinating aspects of the New World Order. It is one of the many themes explored—some directly, some tangentially —in these dispatches. *Dispatches from a Borderless World* defines and explores a Canadian's perspective—one mongrel Canadian's perspective —on the process of global integration that is becoming a defining future of our age.

The task of charting and interpreting the emergence of a New World Order is far too complex to be captured in one volume, and certainly impossible for one person. In these dispatches, we see the beginnings and foundations of identities, encounters, and explorations that will shape our collective future.

Identities

"Who are you?"

The answer to this simple yet profound question takes many forms in a borderless world. Do we define ourselves as individuals or as part of a collective identity? Do we define ourselves by ethnicity, citizenship, and racial origin?

In Canada, perhaps more than in other countries, the fundamental question of identity has many answers. In accommodating the diversity of the world, Canada has bound itself to a momentous human experiment, a constructive exercise in living together. A Canadian identity, both individual and collective, offers a fascinating foundation for explorations and encounters in a borderless world. These Dispatches begin with the search for identity within the evolving Canadian experience.

Becoming Canadian in Tokyo

Tokyo, Japan, 12 October, 1997

The speech was over, the premier was gone, and I was running late for my next appointment. Yet I couldn't tear myself away from the grand lobby of Tokyo's New Otani Hotel. I once left a life here, twenty-nine years ago, and I had never been back.

The New Otani was a way station, our one stop on the journey from Calcutta to Vancouver. It really was new, in April 1968. I was twelve years old. My dad had gone to Canada four months before. I arrived in Tokyo with my mom and infant sister the day Martin Luther King was shot; the week Pierre Trudeau became prime minister. I didn't know it then, of course, but the moment I left the New Otani for the airport was the last, definitive good-bye to my old life: nothing would ever be the same again.

We walked out onto the runway, made the long climb into a Canadian Pacific DC-8: two seats at the back of the plane and a place to attach my sister's bassinet. My emotions were so mixed: a sense of adventure, the anticipation of seeing my dad, and an absolute fear of the unknown.

All those memories surged back last week as the Canadian Airlines Boeing 747-400 touched down. When I left Tokyo in 1968, I had absolutely no idea where life would take me: I was a boy at the cusp of adolescence, still waiting to be shaped.

Back then, the Government of Canada knew me as a name and number on a visa yet to be stamped. Now, the Canadian Embassy in Tokyo had a full program of meetings and interviews arranged for me.

On that whole turbulent journey, from boy to middle-aged man, from Indian to Canadian, from an unformed mind to a life as a writer, Tokyo was a point of reference. It acquired almost a mystical weight for me: I really wasn't sure whether I ever wanted to go back—as though the very act of returning to Tokyo would somehow unravel my life, make everything that happened in Canada an illusion, send me spinning back to some unwelcome past. Standing in the New Otani's lobby, I came face to face with that feeling. And to my surprise, I found an abiding sense of peace. So now, Tokyo is not a talisman but a city: a splendid city that engages the senses. I wonder now I waited so long to return.

Nothing quite prepares you for the shock of meeting Tokyo prices. The eleven-dollar cup of coffee in the hotel sent me rushing into the bright neon maze of the Akasaka district, with new surprises in every window.

Want to take some flowers home? A nice arrangement runs about one hundred dollars, although you can get a basic bouquet for forty-five dollars. A little flowering plant instead? Well, here's a Christmas cactus in a fifteen-centimetre pot for fifty dollars. That's also the cost of a large pizza in one of the many restaurant and food-stall windows adorned with perfect plastic replicas of their fare. In a really basic place, you can get a pizza for one with no extra toppings for fifteen dollars. A bowl of noodles from a four-seat hole-in-the-wall counter runs about eight dollars.

But there are things that don't cost money to enjoy. Walking around is a feast, and it seems faster than driving. Tokyo is amazingly green, and the early morning air on Thursday before the traffic begin is filled with the aroma of damp leaves. The sun feels gorgeous, the fall breeze sweeps away the exhaust fumes, and the life on the clean and ever-crowded streets is a treat to watch. And I still find here what other huge and crowded and costly cities have lost: an exquisite courtesy, the kindness of strangers, and an innate sense of harmony and balance to life. It is easy to find in Tokyo a sense of the future, of splendid technological marvels rooted in a city that has not forgotten people are meant to live, not merely survive.

On Thursday evening, I slipped out of a reception to find a quiet moment in the fourth-floor rock garden at the exquisite Canadian Embassy. The vast concrete plaza captures Canada's spaces; slabs of stunningly cut rock rise from it, giving a sense of majesty that is better experienced than described.

It is a perfect evocation of our country. On that terrace, cooled by an evening breeze, I felt an overwhelming serenity, almost a physical sense of belonging to Canada, to the land as much as to the people. And I knew at that instant my journey is complete. It is an astonishing emotion, and I had to come back to Tokyo to find it. And I know now this city will always be a milestone in my life.

Why we are a most distinct society

Edmonton, Alberta, 29 June 1997

"I 'll be in Newfoundland for most of the summer," said one of my dearest friends, offering baie-qu'appelle preserves to spoon on the ice cream. "You really should come out this year." One of these years, I will. She has been to India with me, but I've never been to Newfoundland with her. Over the years, I have come to know Canada's most distinct society through her. Through family, friends, music, stories and, above all, food. I've developed a taste for cod tongues, but not for flipper pie. And after years of jams and chutneys and sauces, I'm waiting for that perfect summer day when I'll have my first taste of fresh baie-qu'appelles straight from the bush.

In the more than twenty years since we met at university, we've built a cherished friendship—a friendship that's only possible because we both live in Canada. I can't imagine another country where we might have done so, with such freedom and such social latitude.

One of Alberta's great charms is that there are relatively few social strictures to adhere to, no meddlesome rules about who you can and can't mix with. Her trips "home" are a grand event. I know she'll always come back with a trove of new stories, and my nephew—the best-travelled eight-year-old I know—will have his own set of adventures from Newfoundland.

This year, she had a prime seat for the recreation of Giovanni Caboto's landing. And on Canada's 130th birthday she'll be in the place where modern Canada really began, five hundred years ago, with the permanent arrival of Europeans.

Ever since that epochal landing, the arrival has never stopped. In ceremonies across the country on Canada Day, people with a rainbow of origins will swear allegiance and become Canadians. On its 130th birthday, Canada is still a new country, because it never stays still: the definition of the word "Canadian" is ever-changing, altered every time a newcomer becomes a citizen.

"For the first eight years, I really hated this country," says a friend who fled Chile "just to be alive." He was a political refugee from the Pinochet regime, waiting to go back. "We didn't want to stay here, so I didn't even bother trying to learn the language. I didn't fit in. Man, I had a lot of anger."

After eight years of Canadian exile, he took his family back: first to Chile, then to Argentina. "After our first week in Chile, I knew it was a mistake. I didn't belong any more. We couldn't wait to come back to Canada." Now, "I love this country. I don't want to live anywhere else."

Instead of trying to fit in in Canada, he has learned to make Canada fit him. His life here includes some of the best things about his old life in Chile. Apart from an occasional shortage of *pisco*, the vivid brandy of the Andes, "I have everything I want here."

Another friend left France for what he calls the simplicity and anonymity of Canadian life. "Everything is so straightforward here. The people are direct and open. You can do anything you like, having your own life." He grew up in France's wine country, living in the landscape tourists pay thousands of dollars to enjoy, yet he chose to immigrate to Alberta. It wasn't just to look for new opportunities, but also to escape the stagnant life of a country burdened by history and tradition. "I come from la Vendée," he says. "We remained loyal to the king during the revolution." The consequences of that two hundred-year old decision are felt today, in the attitudes and outlook of the people. In Alberta, he finds the pleasure of living in a society and a country that is still being made.

"My dad never went back," recalls a friend whose father left Italy to settle here after the war. "He had a hard time there. I went over lots of times, but the old man, never."

We met when my family came to Canada twenty-nine years ago, and we've been friends ever since. It seems like just the other day his six-year-old son used to come to soccer games with us: the six-year-old who is now a young man in his twenties, flourishing in the family business.

Our lives are really nothing without our friends. And because of Canada, we are fortunate enough to build friendships that introduce us to different ways of life, different ways of experiencing the world, the richness of faraway cultures. This shared human experience, so enormously rewarding, is perhaps the greatest gift Canada offers. It's worth cherishing, as we raise a toast: Happy Birthday, Canada.

Why must my government see me?

Edmonton, Alberta, 22 February 1998

I t used to hurt, when I was growing up in this city, to hear someone call me a "Paki" or a "rug-rider." It hurt less when I grew up enough to understand those comments reflected the abusers' own deeply rooted insecurities, and their fear of the unknown.

No matter how I try to think it through, I can't overcome the stigma of my government labelling me a "visible minority." They're counting just how many "visible minorities" there are in this country, and how many "visible minority" people were born in this country. I can just envision some insecure sociopath preparing right now to "do something" about the fact "those people" now make up a third of the population in Toronto and Vancouver. I find it so cheapening, so fundamentally destructive to my own, broad definition of the word Canadian. To me, Canadians come in rainbow colours, from many vivid ethnicities, from many rich traditions of the human experience. It is this very diversity, and our ability to weave a communal life from it, that makes Canada's civil society one of the most appealing in the world.

When my government calls me a "visible minority," it challenges my definition of what makes me a Canadian. In fact, it implies I'm not a Canadian at all—it feels it necessary to point out in an institutional manner I'm fundamentally different from other Canadians. It under-mines one of my basic aims—to enlarge the meaning of the word "Canadian" to include every citizen of this country. Frankly, I'd rather be called a "rug-rider" than a "visible minority." The straightforward insult is easy to ignore. The government-led assault on my Canadian identity is much harder to deal with.

I accept the government started counting "visible minorities" with some modicum of good intention, as a mawkish way of advancing the status of minorities in Canada. But that still doesn't make it right. If it's true that minorities face discrimination, or need extra measures of pro-tection, we might be better served with a different filter. Rather than "visible" minorities, why not single out "audible" minorities?

Think about it. After a generation or so, nearly all immigrants speak one of the national languages with a mainstream accent. The biggest bar-rier to employment, it seems to me, is the inability to function well in English or French. An inability to speak fluent and idiomatic Canadian English is more of a barrier than skin colour, isn't it? If it's not, I really don't know my country as well as I should. Mind you, maybe skin colour is an over-riding barrier in the minds of the federal government. When one looks at employment patterns, one sees that the private sector pretty well reflects the face of Canada. Without a formal quota program, without counting heads and numbers, without dividing people into sev-eral hundred cubbyholes, the private sector manages to offer employ-ment to people from every background. Granted, there may be resistance in gaining promotions, in gaining the best jobs, or even in landing that all-important first job. But those barriers are small when compared with the federal public service. By the government's own admission, and the use of its own race-based population breakdowns, the federal govern-ment doesn't come close to reflecting the reality of the country: its offices are more monochromes than rainbows. And every year, federal officials wonder where they've gone wrong, and how it is the private sector does much better in employment equity.

Maybe the government should look at the status of audible minorities. There may be a handful of private sector employers who discriminate on skin colour, but I suspect most put the employee's ability to communicate much above the employee's pigmentation. The advantage of looking at the problems of audible minorities is that you can do something about it—help people come up to the level of communication they need to get the jobs they're best suited for. But there's nothing to be done about skin colour. Using the filter of "visible minorities" excludes the hapless Bosnian refugee who speaks neither French nor English, because she happened to be born with peach- or olive-coloured skin. Yet it includes the Honourable Harbance Singh Dhaliwal, Canada's Minister of National Revenue, who happened to be born with brown-coloured skin. Who is more in need of inclusion, and any special assistance that might be needed to enable full participation in Canadian society? By listening to "audible minorities," the government can track the progress of the Bosnians, the Somalis, the Russians—all the first-generation newcomers who need help settling into a Canadian life.

That's why I worry terribly about the whole mentality of dividing Canadians into many subcategories of "visible" minorities. It's an inescapable fact that people have different pigmentation. But shouldn't our government, of all institutions, be colour-blind? Does anyone in the federal government pay heed to Martin Luther King's declaration that he would like his children to be judged not by the colour of their skin, but by the content of their character? Will I ever have the luxury of becoming an "invisible" minority in the eyes of the state, as I am in the eyes of my friends and colleagues? I long for the day my government will look at the author's picture on this book and say: that's a Canadian face.

Why my Canadianism includes Quebec

Montreal, Quebec, 13 October 1996

S ome people seem unable to separate Quebec from its political leaders. It's not easy, when you see Lucien Bouchard on the television screen, to remember there's a whole world beyond the political and intellectual classes, a world full of people whose ancestors called themselves Canadian long before Confederation.

Even so, I'm offended by glib dismissals—we don't need Quebec, better to let them go, why should we put up with their demands—from people who seem to have made no effort to enjoy Quebec, to make friends there, to become intimate with a society that really is different if not distinct. Like it or not, Quebec is a singular society. But I've never seen enough of a difference to make me believe Canada would in any way be better off without Quebec—or that the differences are great enough to justify breaking the country.

I feel at home in Quebec. I always have, no matter how long the gap between visits. And it's not just because I love the French language and the many cultures it represents. In ways I can't quite express, Quebec to me is as essentially Canadian as any other place I've visited in our country.

That's especially true of Montreal. I've never felt foreign in North America's great francophone city, as I have when I'm outside Canada.

This too is home, as diverse, as interesting, and as cosmopolitan as any of the world's great cities. It felt like home in 1972, on my first visit— I was a sixteen-year-old crossing Canada alone by train. I hardly spoke a word of French, yet on my very first walk down Sherbrooke Street, I felt as though I belonged.

It certainly felt like home on a snowy January night in 1995, only months before the referendum, when a furious blizzard blanketed Montreal. It took nearly an hour to get from downtown to Outremont, the cab slipping more than a few times on slushy hills. I set out for dinner with my friend John Goddard, walking through the snow along with dozens of other people—why let a faceful of snow stop Saturday night?

When it was too cold to walk any farther, we found a Peruvian restaurant where a full dinner—corn-and-pepper salad, grilled mackerel and fruit—cost the princely sum of ten dollars each. There was a reasonable selection of wine; every bottle cost thirteen dollars. It was packed; it was noisy, bubbling with conversations in at least three languages. And no one was talking politics. They had real lives, and this is the way Montrealers spend Saturday nights. If Friend Lucien had walked in with a scowl, he would certainly have been offered a glass of wine. But I'm sure somebody would have asked him to chill out if he had started talking about politics.

We went for a coffee and a cognac at one of Goddard's neighbourhood cafés, where we were welcomed like members of the family. It was nearly full—it was only 1 A.M., after all—but they found us a table. They didn't mind that we stayed for a couple of hours, even though we didn't order food, and there were others looking for a place to sit.

When I followed all the coverage of the referendum, there was no talk of the small pleasures of a Montreal Saturday night, no evocation of what it's like to walk within the walls of Quebec City with someone you love, no description of the Edenic beauty of the Cantons de l'Est. Instead, there was confrontation and grimness, one hard demagogue after another. There was not a hint of the Quebec I began to love twenty-five years ago, the Quebec that opened a whole new world of experience.

I'm in the media, so I'm partly to blame. I really didn't do my part to take people beyond the political posturing, to try to explain why I'm so profoundly attached to francophone Canada. When I saw my friend Richard Massicotte last December, he said he voted for sovereignty in the referendum, just to shake things up. The status quo was stifling, he said, and something had to be done to get anglophone Canada's attention. I wondered whether I might have done the same, had I lived in Quebec.

Instead of attention, the referendum experience seems to have produced something much more sinister—indifference. I'm saddened by the people I know who say they can't be bothered about Quebec—stay or go, they say, just make up your minds once and for all. I really fear we might lose our country by indifference. Not by an act of anger, or of passion, but simply because we no longer give a damn. I really wish I could find a magical way to introduce Alberta to Quebecers—not the politics, but the land and the people—and Quebec to Albertans.

We fight hardest for what we love. Right now, there don't even seem to be enough people who care, let alone love.

Rosa Luxembourg meets the
Quebec Lottery

Hull, Quebec, 17 August 1997

D ining outdoors in Ottawa on a breezy summer evening is one of
the pleasures of life in the capital. Some time during the wine,
talk turns to the great tourist draw of the summer: the comprehensive
exhibition of Renoir's portraits at the National Gallery of Canada. "Do
you want to see great art in a bizarre setting?" asks my friend. So we find
ourselves on the way to Hull, to a bunkerlike cube illuminated with
floodlights, set in a sea of cars.

It is the new casino, where the government entices suitably dressed
taxpayers to cough up some more money, with the promise of a chance
to win an instant rebate. The casino resembles the mock-triumphal style
of Mussolini's public buildings in Genoa, an immense block with water-
works and banners adorning the grand entrance, altogether a quite overwhelming expression of the power of the state.

But we are not here to yield our earnings to the Quebec government
a quarter at a time. This retro-fascist monolith is also home to a singular
work of Canadian art. Considering what the National Gallery has paid
for works by well-known Americans, the Quebec lottery corporation
scored a bargain: a monumental work by one of Canada's greatest artists
for about one million dollars. With no sense of irony, they installed all

fifty pieces of Jean-Paul Riopelle's *Hommage a Rosa Luxembourg* in the Hull casino—quite a place for homage named after the celebrated agitator who spent 1918 trying to supplant the German monarchy with a Bolshevik revolution.

Even with the clouds of noise and the flash of slot machines, it is easy to be overcome by the power of Riopelle's work. The mark of great art is its ability to arouse feelings you cannot put into words, to impart meaning at a level that cannot be properly reflected in writing or speech.

Riopelle's homage is a dreamlike construct. It moves from simplicity to complexity, from stillness to turbulence and back again, from ignorance to insight, from indifference to compassion. In traversing the length of this enormous triptych, in trying to comprehend each of the linked panels that comprise the work, you come to see the unfolding of a human life. No ordinary life, no dullard's existence, but an absorbing, tumultuous life in which sorrow and fulfilment are intermingled.

Riopelle's work imparts a profound feeling of redemption. It offers the sense of serenity that most often comes from people who have tasted the best and worst of the world, who have confronted their weaknesses and made the most of their strengths, survived the battle with the twin demons of ego and greed, and at last made peace with themselves.

Rosa Luxembourg met a violent end at the prime of her life: long before her passions were spent, while her shining intelligence made her a natural leader of women and men. Her words, her actions, her very presence made her a threat. And had she not been murdered in January 1919, she surely would not have survived the advent of Hitlerism fifteen years later.

The supreme irony is that the casino embodies everything Luxembourg and her Spartacist movement opposed: naked greed, the exploitation of working people by cynical pursuers of profit and power.

As one moves across the triptych, the eye travels from the vague avian shapes of the opening panels to the tumult and clash of the middle ones and the final images rooted in lyricism and calm. And there, just when the eye moves off the last panel, is the entrance to a bar called Banco.

The costly bar, the one meant for the successful gamblers who have risen above the ruined dreams of the gaming floor far below.

The absurdity is almost too much to bear. But there is more. On the way out, I notice a large acrylic box full of contest entries. Win twenty-five thousand dollars, it says, by counting the number of white geese in Riopelle's work. Geese? White geese? Is that what Riopelle intended those ephemeral birds to be? And which ones are geese, exactly, in that dreamscape of birds? Judging by the entries, thousands of gamblers have been through Riopelle's homage: not to understand, not to experience, but to simply count what looks to them like white geese. It's like running a contest to see who can most accurately count the number of times Shakespeare uses the word "prithee" in his plays.

It is a fitting conclusion to this bizarre exposition. By making Riopelle's homage the object of a contest to count the birds, Loto Quebec defines why the casino exists. Is there really a difference between stripping the meaning and context from Rosa Luxembourg's life and Jean-Paul Riopelle's art, and stripping meaning and context from the lives of the ordinary people who are invited to abandon prudence and judgement at the casino door?

The shore where Canada was born

Niagara-on-the-Lake, Ontario, 27 April 1997

Even on an overcast April Sunday, when the frosty air clings to you like an unwelcome attention, the riverside farms of Niagara-on-the-Lake are among the most alluring places in the world. Just to the west, along the Niagara Parkway, stands the monument to Major General Isaac Brock who on 13 October 1812 died while repelling the American invaders who sought to claim this escarpment as their own.

On this riverbank, from the lakeshore to Queenston Heights, that pivotal act of resistance gave birth to our country. It was the act of national bonding that made Confederation possible; the first time Canada became something other than a patchwork of colonial settlement. To look across that ribbon of water now is to marvel Canada ever came to be, that the notion of such an unlikely country, spreading east and west above the United States, fired the imagination of generations of settlers and immigrants.

What is our country if not an act of imagination? What is it rooted in but a shared resolve to create and sustain something larger than the sum of us? From anywhere on the vineyards of the Inniskillin estate, indeed anywhere on that stretch of the parkway, the perspective is the same: the vivid green of the riverbank, the becalmed downstream flow of the Niagara River, and another country on the opposite shore.

From this vantage, so near it is like another neighbourhood in this pastoral landscape, all the eye sees is the country of American nostalgia. The neat houses, the flags, lawns running to the very edge of the bluffs: the America Walt Whitman sang 125 years ago. It is irresistible, its very placidity a magnet. How then did we resist the pull? It would be so easy, so very easy, to abandon all pretence of our differences, to cross the river for good, to join our fate to theirs once and for all.

But we don't. Nor did all those Canadians who lived before us, who for generations nurtured and shaped the idea of a country that would grow to become today's Canada. What was the impulse that drove Upper Canadians and Lower Canadians, feuding and divided as they were by language and sectarianism, to band together as one to resist the American invasion? What was it that made anglophone Canadians feel closer to francophone Canadians than to the anglophone Americans who sought by force to join our country to theirs?

This very peninsula, this very riverbank, gave birth to the notion of a country, of the Canada that was at last created in 1867. And the most remarkable achievement, on our side of the river, was to sow the dream that travelled the world: to make Canada a place people of all origins yearned to settle.

Still the wonder endures. For immigrants, America was at least as compelling a destination as Canada. Both shores of the river, the New York bluffs and the Canadian flats have their share of citizens whose origins lie in far-off lands. How is it this intimately shared geography, each shaped by generations of newcomers, yielded such different countries? Perhaps Canada is an act of faith, a belief not so much spoken as held in our hearts, that our country is a mighty human accomplishment, an idea compelling enough to resist the natural pull of geography.

To follow the meander of the Niagara River from the falls to the lake is to understand all too vividly how history might have taken a different turn. Had Brock failed, Upper Canada might have become part of the muscular expansion of the United States. It would have been so very easy to fail, and it is a marvel the Americans did not keep on trying to seize the territory that lay within their sight, if not their grasp.

We understand, too, our country remains a fragile creation. We see the pressures and the fissures daily. Not just separatism in Quebec, but resentment in every part of the land. There are even some Canadians who genuinely believe the country is finished—that we might be better off were Canada to break into smaller, more efficient parts.

When you stand amid the Inniskillin vines, looking beyond the sere vinestocks at the barren trees, the spring grass, and the river beyond, you recall the resolve of those Canadians from a bygone age who fought to build a country here.

A few kilometres upstream, the Niagara River tumbles across ice-clad rocks in a thunder of spray and foam: but on this bank, there is no sign of the violent journey of so placid a stream. And you wonder: can the idea and ideals of Canada be so readily quelled by those who want our country diminished or sundered?

A view from the other tribes

Edmonton, Alberta, 12 February 1996

I really can't believe the ease with which so many people discuss the destruction of Canada.

St. Albert MP John Williams is typical. There he was the other day, reducing the future of the country to a choice as casual as buying a tin of soup. Either Quebec stays or it goes, he said. If it stays, it has to choose equality. Otherwise, it can go. Is it just a matter of semantics, or what? When an MP doesn't understand Quebec's constitutional position is all about the search for equality, simply that, what is one to think?

I would feel better, I suppose, if such clotted thinking were a rare instance. But I hear far too much of such talk. The stay-or-go argument has a simplistic appeal. Does no one stop to think the "go" argument means the end of Canada? No, I don't want to hear all that stuff about how the rest of the country would do better, hang together, and so forth. When you hive off a large chunk of a country, that country withers.

In the calamitous event of secession, there may be an entity called Canada somewhere in the ruins. But it will not be the country we have today. And believe me, nothing we build from the ruins will be as special, as civil, as appealing, as the Canada we live in now.

Maybe there's a wider problem here. When we reduce the Quebec question to its essence, we see how tribal it is. It's about people who came from the British Isles and people who came from France. Where does that leave the rest of us? We are the Other Canadians, ten million strong, who are of neither British nor French descent. In a fundamental struggle for the future of our country, we are largely outsiders. When was the last time one of the Other Canadians had a decisive part in the fight? Never. The Prime ministers of the last thirty years have been either British or French. In fact, the British have been all too content to leave the fight to the Federalist French and the Separatist French.

We Other Canadians might see a Hnatyshyn as governor-general, or a Klein, a Ghiz, and a Romanow as premier, but we're shut out entirely from the two roles—prime minister of Canada and premier of Quebec —that are at the heart of this tribal struggle. Heck, forget the top jobs. When was the last time the federal government actually entrusted one of us Other Canadians with a portfolio that dealt directly with national unity? When did the civil service teams that carry out the actual negotiations include a due representation of Other Canadians?

Here we are in Edmonton, the most ethnically diverse city in Canada (73 per cent of the population is neither French nor British), utterly helpless to intercede in the tribal struggle that's beyond us. When our ancestors or we came to this country, none of us Other Canadians understood this poisonous division, this potential for the destruction of Canada. I have yet to meet an Other Canadian who takes Canada lightly, or for granted. When you come here from somewhere else, or have a family memory of coming here from somewhere else, you value and cherish everything you have.

Maybe the British and the French have fought too long, so long that real compromise and consensus is no longer possible. If that's so, then it's up to Other Canadians to champion the country we have adopted and love. All of us made a choice: We chose Canada. This is our country and we have no other. While the tribal adherents shout their slogan of "stay or go," it is up to Other Canadians to develop the compromise, the accommodations necessary for our country to survive and flourish. In one sense or other, all of us Other Canadians are a minority.

Can we not use experience to help our fellow citizens to understand how that feels? To look with some empathy upon six million francophone Quebecers trying to maintain their place in a continent of some 280 million anglophones? Do we not understand better than anyone else does what it means to be a distinct society? That it is a simple quest for respect and dignity, not a "special" right to allow us to lord it over others?

The British and the French are entrenched. We Other Canadians are a third force in the country, a country that may die if we are complacent. If we don't speak up for the Canada we embraced, who will?

How a shy Canadian invented the future

22 November 1998

By the sixth or seventh photograph, his is the first figure to catch my eye: the slender Canadian with an elegant moustache and a shy half-smile, his gestures bespeaking politeness and deference.

In some photos, a wisp of smoke curls up from a cigarette in his right hand—always the right hand, because by now I have noticed the empty left sleeve tucked into a suit pocket, or pinned elegantly below the shoulder.

From his private diaries, from the stiffness and formality of his public memoirs, a shining intelligence emerges. Within the intelligence is an enigma—there is no mention of his childhood as an orphan (his father died when he was thirteen months old, his mother when he was eleven); no mention of how it is that he has only one arm (a mishap with firecrackers when he was six; the infected arm didn't heal despite skin grafts and had to be amputated). There is no gold mine here for a biographer or a novelist; the image he wished to leave for history is so carefully constructed that it is virtually inscrutable.

Yet he continues to provoke my curiosity; the very reticence of his writing makes me wish I had met him, even heard about him, before he died in March 1995, a few weeks short of what would have been his ninetieth birthday. Now, after learning what I have learned, I am ashamed to say that until this year I knew nothing about John Peters Humphrey, the man who invented the future—or at least, a model of how the future ought to unfold.

He is the hero Canadians don't know: the New Brunswick orphan who grew up to become one of the world's foremost advocates of human dignity, the chief architect of the Universal Declaration of Human Rights.

Yet the name of John Peters Humphrey is well known among those who champion the rights and freedoms of ordinary women, children, and men the world over.

In Ottawa last September, South African President Nelson Mandela called Humphrey "one of those rare men and women who make the world the theatre of their operations. "As an architect of the Universal Declaration of Human Rights, he became a citizen not only of Canada, but also of the world."

The future that Humphrey evokes is based on shared values: compassion, nonviolence, justice, respect; it is a call to live together in joy, not merely to tolerate. Humphrey wants us all to remember that we are sisters and brothers, that we are bound by blood, that beneath the self-imposed divisions that divide us is the binding experience of being human.

It is a future that may never arrive. But it exists—in an idealistic, even Utopian form. It is there to discern for all whose minds and hearts are graced with clarity: a model for how the world can live together without rancour, oppression, aggression, and hatred. Moving through the words to arrive at the essence and meaning of Humphrey's work is a humbling experience. It is as though the teachings of Mahatma Gandhi and apostles of peace before him have been distilled into one workable document that will have the force and effect of law. It is a legal, but not legalistic, code of ideal conduct for humankind.

The vision Humphrey set out half a century ago was finally moulded into what we know now as the Universal Declaration of Human Rights.

Humphrey was a law professor at McGill University when he was asked in 1946 to become the first director of the human rights section of the United Nations. It was there that he worked on the declaration, which was adopted by the United Nations on 10 December 1948.

Eleanor Roosevelt, the American who chaired the UN Human Rights Commission, called it a "Magna Carta for the world." But characteristically Canadian in his modesty, Humphrey was reluctant to claim credit for his accomplishment. Indeed, much of the credit went to the French diplomat Rene Cassin, who rewrote a final draft of thirty articles from Humphrey's work and was awarded the Nobel Prize for peace for his effort. Humphrey did not protest, saying the document had been written by humanity and human experience: he was just the one who pulled it together.

Humphrey was awarded the Order of Canada in 1974. This year, Canada Post issued a stamp in his honour.

Mandela paid tribute to the declaration, saying: "For those who had to fight for their freedom, such as ourselves, it is encouragement and vindication for the justice of our cause."

When will that vision of global freedom and justice be fulfilled in history? Humphrey never lived to see it. He was my age, forty-three, when he drafted an international bill of rights in his role as director of the United Nations human rights division. In every subsequent year of his life, the world saw new violence, new bloodshed, new intolerance, new oppression, bred by the old hatreds.

I wonder whether his optimism dimmed with the passing of years. And it's my turn to wonder: if I live to be his age, will I ever see a day when the promise of the Universal Declaration is largely fulfilled?

As I write, the blood of democrats soaks the soil of my beloved Indonesia. The present government of India, the country of my birth, spends far more on nuclear weapons and military prowess than on education and health care, the real building blocks of civil society.

My own country, Canada, continues to talk the rhetoric of human rights while the prime minister puts trade and business first; the finance minister insists we are in better shape than ever as food banks blossom and children awake cold and malnourished in our land of enormous bounty.

No, that future is not in sight. Even so, it is the offered promise of the Universal Declaration that saves me falling from hope to despair, and especially that final fall into the corrosive pit of cynicism.

It sometimes startles me to realize I am becoming more of an idealist and optimist as I grow older, while many of my acquaintances are going in the other direction—my cynical teens and twenties now seem a lifetime away. And it seems strange to me that my sense of hope continues to burgeon as I encounter so much more of the sadness and injustice of the world.

Perhaps I can perceive more clearly now the elusive quality that helps people through their suffering, convincing them that they will indeed live to see a better day. Perhaps it is the feeling—not logic, just feeling—that Humphrey's dream may yet be fulfilled, if we can change the attitudes of those with power. In the history of ideas, half a century is, after all, a very short time.

What makes a Canadian?

Edmonton, Alberta, 1 July 1995

All across the country today, a shared ceremony carries an extra meaning for a select group of people. On Canada's birthday, after taking a solemn vow, they acquire a certificate of Canadian citizenship. What better day to become a Canadian than Canada Day? The act of citizenship is one of the most profound choices in an immigrant's life. It is the moment you formally, officially, exchange one national identity for another.

Relatively few of the world's 5.7 billion people ever have the chance to choose a new country and fewer still the opportunity to choose Canada. Yet the act of citizenship is only one step in becoming Canadian—Canadian, in the sense of making the new country your very own, in claiming its intimacy, its vital currents, its rhythms. For some people, the transition comes quickly, even easily. For others it can take much longer, even a lifetime here—a life spent thinking about that other bygone place where they were born, perhaps second-guessing their decision to choose a new country and its exotic life.

The act of becoming Canadian is an evolution. There is an undefinable moment when "home" becomes where you are, and that other "home," the one you left behind, turns into a nostalgia for a place as it once was, at a point now vanished in time.

Some of course spend their whole lives with one foot in each world, never quite belonging to either. The home left behind ceased to exist the day they left. It began to change, evolve, and develop without them. The familiar connections of daily life, once severed, cannot be restored. Go back after one, two, three, five years, and there are still similarities—but the home, the place, the family left behind, is no longer exactly as it was. If it is not evident in the life and the growth of the cousins and nieces and nephews, of the brothers and sisters grown to an unexpected maturity, then it is manifest in more subtle ways. The character of the street, the villages, the town, all will have changed in ways that are apparent to all but the wilfully blind.

"*El destierro es redondo,*" wrote Pablo Neruda—exile is like a circle. You keep moving, between countries, between identities, no longer quite belonging in the place you left, never quite at home in the place you come to. Becoming Canadian is a step out of the circle—a decision to stop moving, to stop yearning for what might have been, to accept that this country is your present and your future, that this land is where your roots belong. Having made that decision, you come to the portentous question that can have so many answers—does your new country want to accept you?

No matter how hard one tries to take possession of the word *Canadian*, to broaden the word's definition to include every single citizen of this country, there are subtle and overt signs of rejection, official reminders that people with "differences" don't really belong: they may have a Canadian citizenship, but they aren't really Canadian.

Is there any term more odious than "visible minority?" I absolutely detest being called that. What could be more shameful than to know your country sets you apart on so trivial a basis as the colour of your skin? I don't hear of anyone being called an "audible minority" because of their accent. Yet I am a "visible minority" because my government chooses to underline the fact most Canadians don't share my hue.

Well, what do we call you, the bureaucrat might ask? Government, after all, perpetuates the label "visible minority," and its equally clumsy cousin, "multiculturalism." I have an easy answer. Call me Satya. And if you want to know what to call my people, as in "you and your people," call us the Das family. That's the only collective identity that really fits. If you want to lump me in with any other group, whether on the basis of age, gender, ethnicity, colour, language, income, what have you, the word "Canadian" should suffice—shouldn't it? How much more poetic and apt the words of Desmond Tutu, the description South Africa chose for itself to describe its diversity—the Rainbow Nation. So many different strands coming into one.

The true meaning of being Canadian, surely, is to embrace and celebrate diversity. People who come to that insight always find reward. Don't take my word for it. Ask Pansy Strange, who celebrated her 90th birthday a few days before Canada turned 128. For the past thirty years, Pansy and her husband George, ninety-two, have offered not just a second home but a new family to dozens of Canadians who first arrived here from India. When I asked permission to write about her, she hesitated—she does not wish it to seem as though she is seeking to draw attention to herself. "I've had fifty-one for Christmas dinner," she told me at a recent gathering that included some of her "children" and "grandchildren." The love within that family does not need to be demonstrated. It is evident in every gesture, in the small acts of kindness people do for those they care about. Pansy and George made the act of becoming Canadian all that much easier for those they adopted, and Pansy says their lives have been filled with richness in return.

I cannot think of a more affirming symbol of what Canada ought to mean.

How a CanIndian family tried
to go "home"

Coimbatore, India, 14 September 1996

N arayan Jayabal left this southern Indian city twenty years ago looking for a better opportunity. He went to Germany, to England, and finally to Edmonton, where he made a home. Now, he has come full circle. "Coimbatore is where the opportunity is", he says, and this is where he's going to make his new life.

A decision that sounds so simple is anything but. In the time he was away, Jayabal became a Canadian; both his daughters were raised in Canada. Now that he's a migrant in reverse, the habits and memories of Canada won't let go.

"It's taking some time to adjust, that's for sure," he says, as his chauffeur guides the air-conditioned Tata Estate Wagon down a rough road in a landscape of coconut palms, the Nilgiri hills etched on the horizon.

The return to Coimbatore gives Jayabal the chance to run a company—an opportunity he never had during an engineering career with Siemens in Edmonton. Usha, his spouse, spent fourteen years working for the provincial government. When Jayabal was offered the chance to manage an electrical component plant established by a Canadian-Indian business partnership, the career move was too good to pass up.

Jayabal took the manufacturing plant from design and construction right through to production, which begins this month.

After the province's restructuring, Usha's job in public works was no longer a sure thing. Now, she runs a business of her own in Coimbatore, distributing electrical parts. "We have certainly made the right decision in coming here," Usha says in the family's new living room.

The Jayabals sold their home in Edmonton's River Ridge, and shipped all their belongings here. The walls are full of pictures of Edmonton. There's a souvenir plate from Klondike Days. The Jayabals and youngest daughter Sabrina have been in Coimbatore a year now; Sabrina has just finished Grade 9nine "It's OK," she says, "but it's kind of frustrating sometimes." She goes to a school that teaches both English and French. The other girls "speak English in class, but they speak Tamil outside class," so Sabrina feels left out. The shift is even harder on sister Praveena, who arrived in summer after finishing Grade 12 in Edmonton. Praveena was president of the Strathcona high school students' union, enjoyed track and field, joined a lot of community events.

She's enrolled in a business college in Coimbatore, and after two months of classes, the culture shock hits home. "I'm used to the Internet and Power PCs," she says. "They don't even have the Internet here yet. And the computers they use are real 1960s stuff."

She calls her fellow students' conversation "really immature, like they were still in Grade 7." Praveena finds education here too regimented, emphasizing rote learning, and memorizing "right" answers—completely at odds with her Canadian education.

Praveena, like her sister, is trying to learn Tamil, the language of Coimbatore. But she's far from certain she'll settle here. "This is mom and dad's new home," she says. She might study here for a couple of years, "but I really miss everything back home."

Usha seems startled when Praveena refers to Edmonton as "back home," but the children are resolutely Canadian. They have been to Coimbatore before to visit relatives. Home is where they were born and grew up. Praveena has learned other things of value since coming here.

"We take so much for granted back home," she says. She's struck by how people can live simply yet happily, with only a few possessions. "That's something we've lost back home."

Jayabal and Usha can reestablish roots severed two decades ago but the children have to start afresh. They have names typical of the region, but they have hardly any connection with the language and the culture. Coimbatore has a population a bit larger than Edmonton's, but "there's nothing to do here," Praveena says.

For her parents, it's one aspect of the immigrant dream—to return as a success to the land you left behind. For Praveena, it's an interesting experience of living in a foreign country—just for a while. "Edmonton will always be home."

Becoming Canadian in England

Cambridge, England, January to April 1987

In the 1980s, Britain, the Mother Ship for many Canadians, also became the Mother Ship of the global economy. Margaret Thatcher's fervent adoption of neo-liberal economic policies, soon copied by Ronald Reagan in the United States, laid the foundations of a global economics where the flow of capital overcame most if not all national borders. The search for identity in a borderless world, and the fundamental character of the global economy—the recurring themes of these Dispatches—both emerged during my stay in Cambridge at the height of the Thatcher era.

I travelled there in January 1987 thanks to the bequest left by Lord Nuffield. He gave away the fortune he made building and selling Morris motor cars, and his legacy, The Nuffield Foundation, offered me a Press Fellowship at Wolfson College, Cambridge. This essay is the first of two (the other is on page 97) drawn from a memoir of that time, written at that time.

"Come and tell me how the English misbehaved in India," commanded the lady at the reception. How to respond? She was of eminent status within the community: she was an adult during the last days of the Raj. What did she want to hear from me? Did she not know of the Bengal famine of 1942–43 in which at least two million people died? That this was a man-made disaster, with food appropriated for the war effort? Did she want me to repeat the grim stories of people eating leaves off trees when they had nothing else, lying down to die on the land that should have sustained them? And why ask me, someone from the first generation of independent India? Did she want to know whether I harboured any animosity towards England? Or was she merely trying to make conversation?

Keeping in mind I was a guest in her country, I took the broad historical view. About how every invading force in India had acted with varying degrees of brutality, "misbehaved" to use her term. About the Emperor Ashoka's slaughter of the people of Kalinga, and his subsequent conversion to Buddhism. About the ultimate destruction of the Buddhist civilization by the Hindu revival that began in the second millennium of the Christian era. About the Muslims, the Afghan conquests, the Moghuls. India assimilated them all, I explained. Even the English: the ruling classes of England and India arrived at an accommodation and even an understanding. No one rocked the boat. Feudalism was perpetuated. Injustice followed its preordained course, whether the feudal lords had brown faces or white ones.

"Ah," she said, "But we didn't really assimilate. We left." I didn't want to give offence, and politely agreed. But did she not realize the degree of interchange between the two cultures? How much each had borrowed from the other? That although there were few Englishmen who stayed behind in India, there was thousands who brought India home with them? That the post-independence migration of South Asians to England was a face of assimilation? Or was she deliberately feigning ignorance, to see how I would respond?

•   •   •

I went to lunch at University College, London, with one of Britain's leading psychologists. Dr. Neil O'Connor had met my parents when they were students in London thirty-two years previously. As we went in to lunch, he nodded to Jeremy Bentham, who sat in his chair at one end of the hall. Bentham had been dead for several generations, of course, but requested in his will that he should be stuffed and placed in the college. The taxidermist had done a fine job, and I actually looked to ensure the old boy didn't nod back.

Dr. O'Connor was an expert on idiot savants. He had recently hosted a television show on his work, and remarked on the large number of deranged phone calls he had received in response, "and those were the people with degrees."

He asked me what I had seen so far. I mentioned the hopelessness, the sense of drift, I had seen on so many young faces. I didn't see this lack of purpose among older people, even those who held relatively low-income jobs. Did this have something to do with the war, I asked. Did the people who came through the blitz and struggled through the 1950s have a determination others lack? Different expectations of life? Why did the jobless young seem so particularly dispirited?

Dr. O'Connor and his colleague Dr. Beate Hermeling had come through the war. The experience had confirmed Dr. O'Connor in his communist beliefs—an accepted deviation in England. Just for mischief, he made a point of showing his party card at the border controls, every time he travelled to the United States His communism was more utopian than Stalinist. He held little brief for totalitarian systems. Dr. Hermeling spoke with a rich mid-European accent and asked whether I considered myself someone displaced, or was I truly a Canadian? Or an Indian? Both those, I said, and more: I had been born into an Indian milieu, shaped by a Canadian one, and with all the world's languages and cultures to choose from, adopted the French as the one I most enjoyed. Ah, she said, then you're displaced, like me. And her ideas about the dispirited youth were ones of displacement: these people had been displaced within their own culture. They had little incentive or initiative, little connection with "traditional" English values of work and family, a lack of motivation. Dr. O'Connor too lived in an adopted country, far from his native Western Australia. He saw not only a gap of generations, but also a sense of defeatism that comes from "having given half the world away in a generation." (In 1997, Dr. O'Connor, still a lively researcher in his eighties, was run over and killed by a bicyclist as he emerged from his Richmond home.)

•   •   •

What had I expected from England? What were my perceptions of this country I had never really seen, except for brief stays as a London tourist, and midnight glimpses of channel ports when the night ferry from Paris appeared the most romantic ride in the world? I had never experienced England; never lived here, yet it had been the most formative influence on my life. I spoke its language more fluently than the one I had been born to, grew up in two cultures indelibly shaped by it, took the greatest pleasure in its literature.

Did I expect too much? Why was I surprised by the vivid contrasts between Cambridge's coddled life, and the sadness and misery I encountered in my travels in England? Was it a colonial residue, some subconscious thought that my two countries—Canada and India—were somehow inferior, because England wouldn't have ruled us otherwise?

I remembered the surge of pride I felt that summer day in 1982, when Queen Elizabeth signed Canada's new constitution, and I felt my country was free at last—we had obtained full control of our destiny, no longer subject to the authority of the English parliament.

•   •   •

But England was part of me long before I came to Canada. When I was small, growing up in India, I went to an English-medium school called The Stewart School. We lived in Bhubaneswar, capital of the state of Orissa, and the seat of Utkal University, where my parents taught. The city was an uneasy marriage of old and new. As an archaeological site it is a treasure: fine temples from the eleventh century Hindu renaissance, sacred Buddhist sites, a history spanning three millennia. The "new" capital's buildings, grafted onto the classical city, were a sprawling modern conurbation. The Stewart School was within sight of the twin hills of Khandagiri and Udayagiri, remnants of a Jain monastery that predated the Christian era. I had to learn this from my parents—in our school in independent India; the curriculum was still English. And though we lived among so much history, it was never explained as being part of our culture and tradition.

It was bizarre to live among so much history yet to have it denied in our classroom. My history and physical training teacher, Captain Fernandes, once gave me a prize for a composition: it was a copy of the gospel according to St. Luke. So while living examples of Hindu spiritual thought were around us, we learned to recite the Anglican Lord's Prayer at assembly every morning. The history we learned was of the Moghuls, of their imperial way, as though by teaching us about an older empire our teachers were denying us the experience from whose shadows India had recently emerged.

Our family spent two years in the United States, where my father was a visiting professor, before returning to India. He had a chance to win a tenured professorship at the University of California at Los Angeles, yet he passed it up—he did not want his son to grow up American, and face the draft for the Vietnam War. We came back to Bhubaneswar when I was ten.

•　　•　　•

My first history teacher upon returning to Stewart was an Englishman called Gilbert. He asked me a question. I didn't know the answer. He asked me to extend my hand and slapped it hard with the metal edge of a ruler. He asked me why I didn't know. I answered I had just returned from America. He grabbed my forelock, twisted it until I felt the hair pulling out of my scalp, and called me a liar. I had never felt so humiliated. He found out later what I said was true, yet he never apologized.

Gilbert was due to leave soon, and I thought, in the way a ten-year-old might, of how best my revenge might be gained. I persuaded my parents to let me buy a cheap wallet—one of those common in Indian markets, with wild animals carved into the leather. I put an English penny in it, with a note explaining I had done so to ensure Gilbert would "not be penniless" when he arrived back home. I thought it a grand insult, yet he appeared touched, even moved by the gift. I thought I would never understand the adult world. Did this man not realize I was showing him contempt?

If Gilbert taught me to think ill of Englishmen, Harris taught me that there was an admirable side. Harris arrived shortly after Gilbert left with my wallet and my penny. Harris was a language teacher, appointed by the British Council I believe, and he was the first to recognize I would make my life as a writer. Harris was an inspiration, a judge, and a friend. He read my essay on *The Odyssey* and looked at me with a keen emotion. "Das," he said, "You are like the Bard of Avon. You are the Bhubaneswar Bard." Harris gave me eleven out of ten on my work, a mark he repeated throughout the term. This caused me considerable trouble after he left, for my English mark totalled 110 out of 100. The school authorities—the principal was a large, florid man named Wells—decided I had received ten out of one hundred and simply added the extra digit. It didn't occur to them that even a schoolboy would not utter so nonsensical a forgery. So they used ten as my final mark.

Harris's time in Bhubaneswar was a magical one for me. It was the beginning of what might be called the awakening of consciousness. One day, sometime in the middle of 1966, he drew on the blackboard a chicken-track within a circle. "Does anyone know what this is?" he asked. I felt like venturing that it was a chicken's footprint, yet kept quiet, for I could not understand why Harris would draw something so trivial on our blackboard. "This," he said with solemnity, "is the symbol for nuclear disarmament."

And so it was we learned of the world beyond India, a world apparently threatened by a destructive power greater than any of us could imagine, a threat we could not comprehend, which is why we greeted it with certain schoolboy scepticism.

Harris was the first teacher I regarded as a mentor. I felt I could talk to him, and he would understand me. It was Harris I went to when Lengraj the Hindi master hit me across the eye, causing it to swell and ache. He simply wiped it with warm water and cotton, and muttered under his breath. I told my parents the gate had slammed into my face. Lengraj had hit me because I could not conjugate some verb to his satisfaction.

I do not mine these childhood memories now to show masters were cruel or that I suffered unduly. Rather, they illustrated how much I appreciated the many small kindnesses Harris bestowed upon me, how he taught me to believe in myself, how he set me on my life as a writer, how he laid the foundations of what would one day become my Canadian identity.

Requiem for a clandestine land

Edmonton, Alberta, 22 November 1998

"I love fresh snow," declares Sabah Barzangi, opening the blinds in her north Edmonton living room. "It's just like my home city." Memory clouds her expression: the memory of her city Koya in northern Iraq, in the mountainous land of an ancient people who have never had a country, never had a place where they could live and breathe without fear.

They are the Kurds. Theirs is a history of clandestine identity and a concealed language, a culture perpetuated in hiding, briefs gasps of freedom quickly snuffed out by the marauding, assimilating neighbours who have never allowed Kurdistan to emerge.

Sabah, forty-one, and her husband Jalal, forty-five, are writers. Their poetry, plays, and journalism cost them their safety, and brought them a sentence of death.

"We left everything because we wanted democracy and freedom for our pen," says Jalal, scrupulously choosing the words in English—the strange new language he began to learn after he and his family arrived in Edmonton last 25 February.

If Jalal had agreed to become a propagandist for Saddam Hussein, renounced his people and his identity, he might have remained in Iraq forever. He and Sabah could not even consider such an offer. "Our children are going to be Canadian, Kurdish Canadian," Sabah says with determination.

Yet for five years, from 1991 to 1996, they experienced more freedom than they had ever enjoyed. That was the short life of the Regional Government of Kurdistan, the United Nations-guaranteed territory carved out of Iraq after the Gulf War. The guarantee didn't survive the first real test. When Saddam Hussein's troops invaded in May 1996, the world did nothing to protect the Kurdish enclave.

The Universal Declaration of Human Rights prohibits many of the things that have happened to the Kurds: aggression, rape, torture, imprisonment, various forms of slavery. But there is no one article that covers the theft of a country: or rather, the denial that a country ought to exist.

There are forty-five million Kurds in the world, yet most are not allowed to identify themselves as such. There are more than twenty million Kurds in Turkey alone, yet they are not allowed to openly use their language, nor to perpetuate their culture. If Kurdistan existed, it would be in territory now occupied by Turkey, Iraq, Iran, Syria, and the southern reaches of the former Soviet Union.

As Sabah speaks on a wintry Tuesday morning, her five-year-old son Jwamer is absorbing *Mr. Dressup*, then *Sesame Park*: part of his daily immersion in Canadian culture. He goes to kindergarten and, like his sisters Niga, twelve, and Ewar, fifteen, speaks the Canadian English learned at school. Jalal is halfway across town, learning English.

Two days later, with the afternoon sun gilding the walls, Jalal shows his writing: the three books of poetry that had to be smuggled out and published in Sweden, the daily column he wrote in those five free years. He talks about the explorations of human freedom in the work of the poets who influenced him: St. John Perse, T. S. Eliot, Yannis Ritsos, Vladimir Mayakovsky, Nikos Kazantzakis, the Syrian poet Adonis. "They look around at the world; they speak intimately about emotions."

His first book of Kurdish poetry, *The Dance of the Evening Snow*, was published in Sweden in 1979. Jalal reads from his great pacifist poem

"War", and there seems to be an inexhaustible sadness in his eyes. Published in 1993, this poem was "like an explosion," because it denounced both the aggression against the Kurds and the actions of Kurdish guerrillas, says Sabah.

Sabah tries to translate Jalal's words—her English is better than his—yet the clear, strong emotion in his voice need little translation.

> War destroyed my first morning
> War cast my words in the sea
> War consumed my flowers
> War cries Exile to my soul

The poem continues in this vein, but it will take the gifts of a fine translator to render the entire work into English. Some of the Kurdish words are comprehensible to people who understand Persian, Urdu, Hindi, or the other Indo-European languages of Asia. The language of the Kurds comes from that family; it's entirely different from Arabic.

It is the language derived from the ancient Mesopotamian civilization, which dates to 6000 BC—the Kurds are their descendants. The Greeks knew Kurdistan as Medea, and Kurdish traditions are still rooted in the Medean civilization.

The original religion of the Kurds was Zoroastrianism. That ancient faith spread by Zoroaster—known as Zardasht in Kurdish—originated in Persia and survives today in India. Kurds were converted to Islam by the caliph Ibn Omar, an early follower of Prophet Mohammed, says Sabah. "But I also believe in something of the old religion," which reveres fire as a symbol of the divine light that dispels the darkness within humans and in the world.

Photographs of Navrosh, the New Year ceremony, show children gathering with flowers around a fire. Yet this is an image of a terrible beauty—most of the children are orphans, whose families were murdered in a genocidal campaign Saddam launched against Kurds in 1988.

The Barzangis say the best documented estimates are that 182,000

Kurds were killed, many in chemical weapon attacks, and five hundred communities destroyed. In March 1988 in the village of Holabja, a chemical bomb killed five thousand people in five minutes. These were Saddam's "tests" of the chemical weapons he threatened to use during the Gulf War.

In the five years of Kurdish autonomy, Jalal was director of culture for the region and a founder of a committee for free journalists. Sabah wrote in magazines and newspapers about the rights of women, which she says are nonexistent in Iraq and indeed in most of the Middle East. "The mentality is very fascist."

When Saddam invaded in 1996, all was lost. "We left a big house, a big car, a big job, we left everything," says Sabah. Jalal fled to Turkey, Sabah and the children went into hiding. They paid someone to smuggle them to Turkey. Sabah cannot bring herself to talk about that journey, but it is clear that something terrible happened during their escape. In Turkey, it was too risky to acknowledge they were Kurds. They said they were Iraqi. They spent a year there before the United Nations sent the family to a Canadian exile. This is the shape of exile: a townhouse in Castle Downs, the yet-to-be-filled spaces of a Canadian home, devoid of the toys and clutter of childhood.

"I could bring nothing with me from Kurdistan," says Jalal. All their books and papers were lost. A manuscript novel he sent out with a friend was confiscated somewhere and disappeared. Now, both Jalal and Sabah write pages in Kurdish longhand. If they had a computer, they could use the Kurdish font developed by other exiles. The Barzangis are determined to make the best of Canada. The best feeling, says Sabah, is knowing no one will burst into the house in the middle of the night to take them away. They know they and their children will wake up alive. "Now I am happy," says Jalal. "We can write everything." That freedom "is better than being rich."

Why a comfortable exile is never enough

Edmonton, Alberta, 15 November 1998

Sitting around a cosy living room in northeast Edmonton, a vivacious group of friends is drinking coffee, discussing the "full treatment" received in a faraway land. They talk about the "submarine" and the "barbecue" in an offhand way, sometimes with a wry smile, so casually they might be comparing vacation notes. Yet these are not holiday memories. The barbecue was a metal bed with an electric current running through it. The submarine was a two-hundred-litre oil drum full of human excrement and fouled water. People were tied down to the "hot" barbecue, electrodes on their bodies completing the circuit; had their heads plunged into the submarine until they choked—for the "crime" of supporting a government that challenged the economic interests of a small but powerful elite.

These Canadians friends were all Chileans once upon a time, exiled here in the mid-to-late 1970s. They are exchanging memories of their arrest and torture after the president they elected, Salvador Allende Gossens, was murdered in a military coup led by Augusto Pinochet Ugarte in September 1973.

Allende's murder, they note, came during the twenty-fifth year of the Universal Declaration of Human Rights—the document adopted by all countries in the world as a charter of rights and freedoms for every human on the planet.

Yet few countries have lived up to the spirit, let alone the letter, of the declaration. Now, as countries the world over mark the fiftieth anniversary of the declaration, it remains for many people a promise unfulfilled.

Although the Chileans have come together to relive their terror for a writer's benefit, the gathering has a festive mood. They have been awaiting word of Pinochet's extradition to Spain. And if word had come on this cold Saturday, they'd have been down at Edmonton city hall, celebrating.

"Chileans were victims of a comprehensive violation of the Universal Declaration of Human Rights," recalls Ramon Antipan, doubly persecuted in Chile for his leftist politics and his aboriginal heritage. "Fifty years on, we are still fighting for those same basic rights."

Unlike immigrants who choose to come to Canada, or people who make a deliberate choice to cut off their links to their homeland, Ramon and his friends were expelled. Facing a choice between death, concentration camps and exile, they really didn't have a choice at all.

"The government expelled us by decree. None of us chose to come here."

Orlando Herrera, who can smile now even as he speaks of the "full treatment," has ambivalent feelings about the Declaration. "Do we really have much to celebrate?" "Human rights are entrenched in letters and words, but not in fact."

Adds Ramon: "Are we really achieving what was declared? Or are we just living through the struggle again?"

They are gathered in the home of Reinaldo and Carmen Uribe. The stairwell sports a vivid poster of the Argentine physician Ernesto "Che" Guevara, who became a guerrilla leader in Cuba and was killed aged thirty-nine in 1967, fighting in the mountains of Bolivia. The home is part of a large Chilean co-op established twenty years ago—recreating the atmosphere, if not the reality, of the extended family all of them were forced to leave behind.

"This is what we sold outside the stadium, to survive," says Carmen, passing around engraved metal medallions. The stadium in Santiago, Chile's capital, was where Reinaldo and the other men in the room were taken after their arrest.

Their spouses lined up for hours for word of their husbands. Mario Acuna-Castillo and his wife Lucy had no idea of one another's fate, even though they were only a few metres apart. He was a prisoner inside, recalls Lucy, yet when she finally got through the lineup to ask, "they said 'your husband's name is not on the list, so he must be dead.' Just like that, they said 'he's dead, go home.'"

"This is the first time I am saying these things in English, in front of a group," begins Mario, picking up the story on the inside of the stadium —where he was penned into an eighteen-square-metre enclosure, with about one hundred senior officials and ministers of Allende's government for company.

He pauses frequently to let the emotion subside, as he describes his ordeal. Yet he was lucky not to be among the three thousand who died, by official government estimates, in the weeks following the coup—a figure far lower than estimates by others. And lucky too in being sent to a "model" concentration camp in the high desert of northern Chile. Lucky to be held shivering in a place that was shown to the outside world as a reasonable prison, although his first view of it was "exactly the scene from a war movie" showing Nazi concentration camps.

Unlike most of his fellow prisoners, Mario wasn't expelled from Chile, after the United Nations intervened on behalf of those imprisoned.

Yet Mario, an electrical engineer with the national power company before his arrest, was blacklisted from every job he tried to get. So he chose a Canadian exile, "waiting" as Lucy puts it, "every year to go back as soon as Pinochet fell."

They waited so long that they didn't try to put down roots in Edmonton. It was only five years ago, after a futile attempt to resettle in a Chile irreversibly altered by history and time, that they returned to Edmonton and made the decision to become fully Canadian.

In the interim, the country of their nostalgia had disappeared— seventeen years of dictatorship irrevocably changed the character of the people, of the land, of the very streets and neighbourhoods, even the quality of the air.

"Change the name and places, and the story is the same," says Reinaldo. "I went through something very similar to the others."

Somehow, the collective recounting of torture makes it easier to talk about—a shared experience is easier to relive than a solitary one.

Reinaldo's father was a retired military officer, in "a very different military" than the one Pinochet led to power. He couldn't really comprehend his son's forced exile, and Reinaldo could not go back to attend his father's deathbed. "The psychological torture was the worst," he says.

And while Canada offered refuge—along with Mexico, England, and Australia, it was one of the prime havens for expelled Chileans—it wasn't an easy fit.

"I was so cold, I didn't know how to dress for the winter," Juan Reinberg recalls in Spanish. Because he and his wife arrived here with five children, they weren't able to take the English language courses offered to some of the others. "I had to work right away."

Unable to communicate, he would walk five blocks from the bus stop to his job at a sheet-metal factory. "I didn't understand what the other workers were saying."

His hands were so sore, the cold so horrible, "that I cried. I wondered if I was better off being in jail in Chile."

A copperworks union official in Chile, Juan was tortured and jailed for two years. He too was blacklisted after prison. Now, even though he has made a life of sorts here, he is between two worlds: a Chile of the past that no longer exists and a Canada where he has never quite fit in.

He is the quietest of the group. As others talk, he leafs through a thick report, dog-eared with use: it is the 1977 United Nations documentation of human rights violations in Pinochet's Chile. It is the truth Juan offers, to counter those who say Pinochet was supported by a majority, or that his actions were necessary but relatively mild.

The UN's Spanish is simple and declarative, the horrors detailed in it all the more chilling for the matter-of-fact tone. It sets out the violation of nearly every one of the thirty articles of the Universal Declaration of Human Rights—such basics as free speech, free association, free movement, freedom from arbitrary arrest, the right to participate in government. Quite apart from the illegal detention, torture, and "disappearances," it documents the exit-only passports that carried tens of thousands of Chileans to enforced exile.

The difficulty, though, is that the Declaration does not compel countries to abide by it. It is only a resolution of the United Nations. While its Canadian author John Humphrey regarded the declaration as part of the "customary law" of nations, says University of Alberta constitutional law professor Gerald Gall, there is no authority that forces countries to comply with its provisions.

Laws that evolved from the declaration—international covenants on civil, social and political rights—are legally more binding, but enforcement of human rights laws depends on the willingness of other nations to call violators to book.

That's why Canadians of Chilean origin anxiously await the fate of Pinochet, whom many European nations want to bring to trial. And for the friends gathered at Carmen and Reinaldo's house, one of Pinochet's major crimes is that he destroyed the country of their dreams.

For Ruth Morales, going back to Chile now might be possible but it's pointless. When she left, "I locked my house, just took the three kids and some blankets; I thought we would be coming back." She and her family went to Argentina first, but had to flee when a military government assumed power. Their choices, too, were Canada, England, or Australia. They came here. Yet now that she is a widow, and her children have grown here, there is nothing to go back to. "I was always hoping Pinochet would fall, so I can return."

Yet he didn't fall. And that enforced exile, the long wait to go back, prevented many from accepting that Canada would be their home and their future.

"That sense of not belonging, that's what happens when you are displaced against your choice," says Gloria Luisa Antipan. "The damage is pretty deep."

She and Ramon were young people when they came. They settled well into Canada but kept the memory of Chile alive—so much so that their Canadian-born daughter Gloria feels comfortable in both countries and says she'd like to live in Chile for a while.

"Even if you can connect here, function here, you know it's not really the same," says Gloria Luisa, "it's not your own country."

In a sense, says Ramon, the Chileans forced into exile were robbed of "a dream. We had a dream of a country of social justice," with rights and equality for ordinary people. "We were building that dream; in the third year of the government, Allende was more popular than when he was elected."

The dream was shattered by Pinochet's coup, and many of the exiles cannot let go of what might have been. Now, they see Pinochet's fate as the ultimate test of whether the Universal Declaration of Human Rights really means anything to their lives. They want the former dictator to pay for what was done to Chile. "So many forces are at work to save Pinochet," says Orlando.

And in the fiftieth anniversary of the declaration, Orlando, Ramon, Ruth, Lucy, Carmen, Gloria Luisa, Juan, Reinaldo, and their children hope their adopted country will do all it can to promote the spirit and the letter of the declaration that was to have brought true freedom for every person.

"Even in Canada, the rights are not fully achieved," says Ramon. "Many of the people here have suffered discrimination too. Believe me, I'm grateful for the actions of the Canadian people, for the people who put pressure on the government to enable us to come here. But we had to struggle here too: it hasn't been easy."

Human rights are "constantly in danger, not just in the developing countries," but in western democracies too, says Orlando. If anything, the Universal Declaration is a reminder of how far the world has to go before the rights conferred half a century ago become a reality.

Why peace can be more welcome
than prosperity
Edmonton, Alberta, 22 November 1998

Razia Jaffer thought her husband Nizar was joking when he came home for lunch, as usual, and told her she had half an hour to flee the house.

"I asked him to sit down and have his lunch," she recalls. After all, there was no other indication that anything was wrong on this late September day in 1972. The quiet residential street in Kampala, the capital of Uganda, was as tranquil as ever. "We had just bought that house to raise our family in," and its rooms were crammed with furniture and personal belongings.

Then Nizar told her of people being abducted and women being raped, "my legs felt very very weak, that was it," she says. She was fully convinced when their manservant Patrick—considered "a member of the family"—urged his employers to flee. "He was saying please, please go."

Razia packed "one bag for ourselves and one for the baby," nine-month-old Rahim. Razia was worried, but certain she was coming back to the house—she could not imagine she was about to abandon her home and her comfortable life forever.

Ugandans of Asian ancestry had indeed felt anxious when Uganda's new president Idi Amin declared that Uganda was for black Africans only. Within days, however, they knew Amin meant it—he wanted to make Uganda racially pure, even if it meant the utter desolation of the economy, dominated by Ugandans of Asian ancestry.

The expulsion of Ugandans who weren't black was a comprehensive violation of the Universal Declaration of Human Rights. Deprived of citizenship, property, and the right to live in their country, the Jaffers and others became refugees because their own government turned against them.

"We considered ourselves East African," says Nizar. He was a Ugandan whose grandparents had emigrated from Western India to open businesses. Razia was a Kenyan whose family had arrived in Africa in similar circumstances. They were Ismaili Muslims, part of a global community of cosmopolitan and progressive people who were followers of the Aga Khan, a direct descendant of the Prophet Mohammed.

They never imagined they would have to leave one day, says Nizar. "Once you knew this was your country, you didn't think of going anywhere else."

His grandfather and his father had built successful businesses; Nizar had spent six months in Vienna to learn all he needed to set up a plastics factory. In fact, it was his business travel that took him to Nairobi one day in the late 1960s. Visiting a business with his uncle, Nizar met Razia, who was working in the office. He built up enough courage to ask her out—to a trade fair. She said yes, and they married in 1970.

Rahim, the older of their two sons, was born in December 1971, and they fully expected him to grow up in Uganda and join the family business. It was not to be. By the time of Amin's expulsion decree, the Jaffers had a family business worth six million dollars in today's currency. Then they were told they had ninety days to get out. Everyone in the Asian community tried selling their businesses, but there were few takers.

They thought at first of going to Austria, because Nizar had enjoyed his experience, but Austria wasn't taking Ugandan refugees. When they went to the Canadian high commission, "they very warmly welcomed us." In any case, they thought they would be back in a few months. "We didn't even take our home [ownership] papers," says Nizar.

When police and soldiers started taking Asians away for questioning, the Jaffers—who had fled their house for a cousin's apartment by then—decided it would be better if Razia went back to join her family in Nairobi. The final decision was taken when Nizar's father was arrested and interrogated for a full day before the family secured his release.

Nizar recalls feeling totally desolate after seeing his wife and baby off at the airport in Entebbe. He didn't know it then, but the next time he would see them would be in Vancouver. Razia climbed into the plane with her sister-in-law. "We cried in the plane; we didn't know what was going to happen."

At Nairobi airport, there was a new shock. Razia still had a Kenyan passport, but Rahim was a Ugandan citizen. Ugandans were forbidden from entering Kenya, "they wanted me to send the baby back."

Her brothers made a payment to let Rahim through.

Several weeks later, Razia was on a plane again, carrying a ten-month-old baby who weighed twenty-seven pounds. For a long part of the trip, from London to Montreal, she carried the baby on her lap because the flight was overbooked.

Nizar, meanwhile, had left Uganda on his own, unable to contact his wife before he fled. She expected him to be waiting in Montreal, but he had been sent on to Vancouver.

True to their word, Canadian immigration officials quickly ensured the family was reunited. In Vancouver, Nizar reached for his son, but after two months apart, Rahim wouldn't come to him. "That really hit me."

Life in Canada was bittersweet. "I was rich one day and poor the next," says Nizar. A life as an entrepreneur and company director in Uganda didn't equip him with what Vancouver employers wanted most: "Canadian experience."

After weeks of rejection, Nizar asked how on earth he could gain Canadian experience, if no one in Canada would give him a job? "They would just reply, 'we're sorry we can't help you.'"

Because he had owned a plastics factory, he at last got a job as a warehouse supervisor: the job required someone who could tell the difference between types of plastic. Showing up in a business suit, he found himself sweeping the floor on his first day on the job. He came back home that night and wondered what they had done—had they made a terrible mistake in coming to Canada? "I felt totally, totally lost," Razia says in the cultured accent of people educated in British-style public schools. Even though she spoke impeccable English, "I wouldn't step out of the apartment by myself."

Yet in time, with perseverance, the Jaffers built a good Canadian life. They went into business in Vancouver, and when that didn't go well, they moved to Edmonton in 1980 to enter the meat-wholesaling business. After that, they had a muffin shop. Now, they have a successful Grabajabba franchise on Whyte Avenue.

It's quite a departure from life in Uganda. "I still love that country," says Nizar, but they have made Canada their home.

Rahim, the baby Razia carried out of Nairobi, grew up fully Canadian, and "shocked" the family by deciding on a career in politics, recalls Nizar. The family had been displaced by the machinations of politicians, they thought it best to keep their heads down and literally mind their own business. "I told Rahim, you stick to business; politics, that's a dirty game."

But the family was delighted—none more so than Razia's mother Shirin Mohamed, who "ran around giving everybody a hug"—when Rahim, who became fluent in both French and English, was elected MP for Edmonton-Strathcona in 1997.

"We never imagined anyone in our family could succeed so quickly" in public life, says Nizar. Indeed, it's hard to think of another country where a refugee family would see their baby grow up to become a Member of Parliament (and member of Her Majesty's Loyal Opposition) in only twenty-five years.

When a kiss is more than just a kiss

Edmonton, Alberta, 11 January 1997

Two faces come together in the clear Tuscan light: a white one and a brown one, meeting in a kiss. And in that moment, a new world is born. The kiss shared on-screen by Juliette Binoche and Naveen Andrews—playing a pair of lovers in uniform in the Second World War—is a phenomenal moment in one of the most rewarding films I've seen recently.

You feel lucky indeed when a marvellous book becomes an equally marvellous movie—the same work of art expressed in two engaging but different ways. While much of the meditative quality of Michael Ondaatje's *The English Patient* is lost in the movie of the same name, there are moments of intensity that can only be achieved by filmmaking at its most evocative. And so it was with that heady kiss between the Canadian nurse Hana and the Indian lieutenant Kirpal—the depiction of the act made it more real, more substantial, than its description in words. And so too the sense something entirely new is about to come into the world.

In Ondaatje's book, Hana and Kirpal's love was not to be: it was the right sentiment in the wrong time and the wrong place. It survives in memory, always coloured with regret. Hana makes a solitary life, Kirpal returns to India to become a doctor, have children—and neither forgets. It is a denouement reflected in the reality of many wartime loves between people of sharply different ethnic and racial backgrounds. And it was hardly uncommon in the diverse, multiethnic British Army of the Second World War, where people as different as Hana and Kirpal did indeed meet and serve the same cause. Kirpal became Kip, and served the flag well even though he could not abide Kipling—the act of helping to liberate Europe carried within it a promise of liberation for all the people under the flag of Empire.

The film makes Kirpal and Hana's relationship a transcendent act, a foretaste of the society we live in now. That kiss signals the birth of a new way of living in new societies, one in which a Sikh and a French Canadian can share and nurture a love, take it into the unknown future. As Hana goes north to Florence, the viewer is left with every expectation that she will find Kip, and it is left to us to imagine their future. The film turns away from the regret-tinged scenario of Ondaatje's book and transforms it into a myth of creation: a story of how the new world was born from the war.

It is a myth that fits beautifully into what we know from what we have learned in the half-century since the war, the remarkable coming together of so many cultures, of so many streams of human experience. It is very much a creation myth of the modern Canada. And what could be more fitting than to have a French actor and a British one play Canadian and Indian lovers who might have the possibility of making a life in a world that would become ever more diverse and cosmopolitan? This sense of building a new population for a new land informs the creation myth at the heart of Tom Wharton's novel *Icefields*. In Wharton's vision, the making of our country is woven from some of the oldest strands of human experience.

Here, the act of creation is between an Indian and an Indian: an aboriginal Canadian woman with medicine power, from a people so elusive they may have existed more in legend than in life. She comes together with the servant a British aristocrat brought from India. Their daughter

Sarasvati—after the Hindu goddess of wisdom and learning—becomes the Canadian Sara, whose own life's journey takes her from a frontier existence on the icefields to a leading citizenship in the new community of Jasper.

Such acts of myth-making continue a rich tradition in Canadian art and literature, forming and telling the stories of how we came to be a people and a nation. The old countries Canadians left behind were full of their own stories of creation. The experience of the immigrant arrival has nourished the Canadian imagination through what has been a remarkable half-century of artistic expression. The years since the Second World War mark the time when Canadians established what will be seen as our foundation legends—the symbolic and implicit story of how our country came to be. It's told in poetry, in painting, in sculpture, in dance, in music, in theatre, in novels—and sometimes, in a single cinema kiss.

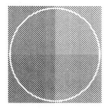

Explorations

The search for identity in a border-less world is by no means a uniquely Canadian challenge. Other cultures, other traditions are coming to terms with defining and developing their fundamental character in a world where the unhindered march of economic integration is building the Global Village foreseen by the Canadian thinker Marshall McLuhan.

Perhaps McLuhan did not expect the tide of the global economy would abet his vision of the communications revolution that makes the world one. In these Explorations, the shaping of identity and experience in other countries and traditions is seen through Canadian eyes—one hybrid Canadian's dispatches, observing the remaking of our world.

The borderless world brings with it all that is beautiful and brutal in the human condition. The Explorations captured in these Dispatches are snapshots: images of people, countries, societies at given moments in time.

Finding hope in a morsel of freedom

East Jakarta, Indonesia, 12 December 1997

"I will always remember this day,'" said my young Indonesian friend. "When I look back, I can say that this was the day it all began."

In many ways, December 12 was an ordinary Friday in Jakarta. Haze in the air, traffic so choked even the twelve-lane arterial roads couldn't cope. A frenzy of noise and motion and all the intensity of life in a sprawling city of thirteen million people. In one vital way, this was a Friday apart. It was the day my friend, and many others like him, sensed something utterly rich and strange: the first stirrings of freedom.

For the first time, there was a tangible feeling that the long rule of President Suharto was coming to an end. No one knows what the post-Suharto era will bring. But my friend is convinced it will mean a sharing of power—if not a full democracy, in some evolutionary form. The patriarch will be gone soon and in his wake will come the end of absolute power.

The feeling began about 1 P.M. that afternoon. The government suddenly announced the ailing president had cancelled a trip to Kuala Lumpur for a meeting of regional leaders. The rupiah plunged, because the government didn't have the wit to delay the announcement until the markets closed. Rumours swept the city that the president was dead; people swore they knew for a fact he had been secretly admitted to hospital. Then came the closure of Sandalwood Street, where the presidential palace sits. As the burgeoning traffic around Freedom Square passed the barriers blocking off Suharto's residence, the rumours gathered weight. They only lasted a few hours, of course, until the president appeared on television to say he needed to rest and recover.

My friend was intoxicated by the taste of freedom in the air. We were sitting in his comfortable suburban living room, fifty kilometres by expressway from his Jakarta office. A few paces away, the indoor garden was open to the summer night, bringing a velvety mist of humidity. His infant son, ignoring the stuffed bear I had brought was playing with the box it came in. His spouse was helping the maid clear the table, while the nanny prepared to take the baby for an evening walk.

This slice of middle-class Asian life, with all its material comfort, perfectly illustrated the Suharto years. He had made all this prosperity possible, but the price was obeisance. Free thinking, alternative ideas, challenges to the governing political order: these were all classified among things not to be done.

For five hundred years, ever since the second Mataram kingdom established itself in Central Java, freedom has been extinct in Indonesia. After the Mataram rulers came the Dutch colonialists. Then came the Japanese occupation during the Second World War. Then the Dutch again, vainly fighting a five-year war to regain control of their former colony.

The very first Indonesian constitution, the first document of "free" Indonesia, deliberately excluded individual rights. Sukarno, who led Indonesia to independence, thought individual rights would intrude on the family- and community-based model of Javanese and Sumatran culture. Soon, Sukarno was banning dissent and dissidents, outlawing parties, stifling opposition. The trend has only continued and intensified under Suharto, to the point that there is no viable opposition.

For my friend, the events of this particular Friday evoked the feeling that his son would grow up in a far different country. My friend was born in 1965, The Year of Living Dangerously, the year Suharto came to power in a bloody civil war that left half a million people dead. Tens of thousands of people suspected of belonging to the Indonesian communist party were slaughtered. My friend hid with his family in a hole dug in their garden, to avoid the rampaging mobs. "My earliest memory is of being in the dark, on my mother's lap, with no one saying a word."

The Suharto years gave him a decent life, a good education, an immense love of Indonesia—and the confidence to criticize and challenge the absolutism of Suharto's power. There are many young Indonesians like him, who want their voices included in the shaping of their country's future. Their main commodities are time and patience. They know the Suharto era cannot last much longer. Above all, that essential human feeling drives them: hope. There may not be any logical reason to think that a more representative government is just around the corner. But such is the power of their hope that they can already look ahead to a future where Indonesia's promise of freedom will at last be fulfilled.

Twilight in Jakarta:
an ailing dictator leaves a nation adrift

Jakarta, Indonesia, 29 December 1997

As President Suharto lies ill in his palace on a muggy December Thursday, the afternoon chaos on Gadjah Mada Street is silenced by the shriek of police whistles and the sound of boots running across pavement. Quickly, dozens of police with riot shields and batons weave through the river of cars and trucks belching black smoke on the clogged street. They force cars aside, open a lane. Then come the trucks carrying black-shirted paramilitary police. First one, then another, then a third. Police tumble out. But they are not carrying firearms. And to anyone who cares to look closely, there seems to be fear in their eyes.

Within moments a chanting, surging crowd spills out of the nearby courthouse. They cry for justice. They shout democracy will not be denied; their day is at hand. They come close to the police, but not close enough to justify force. There is a discipline in this crowd, defying the police to risk a baton charge, or even tear gas. But the police keep their distance. They sense, like the demonstrators, that they are witnesses to a time of change and the old rules of easy repression cannot so readily apply.

In the course of thirty years, Suharto has become Indonesia's absolute ruler. "He is like a banyan tree, allowing nothing to grow underneath," says an Indonesian political scientist.

But now his era is coming to an end. The ruling Golkar party has already nominated him for a seventh term as president come next March, but there is speculation he may not last that long.

"Seventy-six-year-old men die in this country," says a Canadian diplomat. And when Suharto goes, whether now or sometime after next year's election, no one knows what will happen. There is no clear line of succession, no chosen successor.

•   •   •

Indonesia is the world's fourth most populous country and by far the largest archipelago: superimposed on Canada, it would stretch from the westernmost point of the Yukon to the Grand Banks of Newfoundland.

It is never easy to govern—there are always a few simmering rebellions across its breadth. Dozens of Canadian companies have invested billions of dollars in Indonesia, which is emerging as one of Canada's major trading partners. After Suharto, the sometimes-enforced unity of Indonesia might be called into question. Democrats, dissidents, and government loyalists agree that the short-term task of keeping order and some semblance of stability will fall to the army. But no one has an answer for the "what comes after?" The crowd on Gadjah Mada Street has its own kind of answer. They want Megawati, daughter of Sukarno, the Indonesian Republic's first president, to be restored to her rightful place as head of the tamed and constrained opposition.

A few minutes earlier, a court ruling sparked the demonstration. It dismissed a petition by Megawati Sukarnoputri, protesting her ouster from the leadership of the opposition Indonesian Democratic Party by a government-backed functionary. The coup against Megawati sparked riots across Jakarta in July 1996, yet it took a year and a half for her petition to be heard. The judicial panel said it could not find intent of

74

malice. They suggested she appeal to a higher court, or that she launch a civil proceeding against the replacement, and the government.

The crowd running on to Gadjah Mada Street—named after an enlightened prime minister in one of the sultanates that ruled Central Java—dissipates after a few blocks. The change they demand cannot be blocked by court decrees, because they are not the only ones calling for change. Change is being forced on Indonesia by the Asian economic crisis, calling into question the corruption and cronyism endemic in the system.

• • •

The Suharto era social contract—growth and prosperity with no effective opposition or dissent—may unravel in the face of the worst drought in fifty years, mass layoffs among marginal workers, and a crashing halt to the seemingly unstoppable growth of the last decade. For many ordinary Indonesians, political debate is something strange and abstract. "Father [Suharto] has always taken care of us," says a mango vendor in Jakarta's New Market. After his death? "He will find someone to guard the [Indonesian] family." There is no new patriarch in sight—no one who will command that sort of blind faith. Sensing a new era, leading figures within the Indonesian establishment are breaking ranks with the government. "Grassroots people are already aware of their rights and will push their demands for a better life," says one critic of the government. "They cannot be cheated any longer."

This critic is not from a dissident faction, nor from one of the liberal Muslim groups pushing for civil society, certainly not from the socialists and communists who have been banned. His name is Rudini, and he has a significant following within the armed forces that are the guarantor of Indonesia's stability.

Rudini is out of direct power now, wielding indirect influence as head of the Institute of Strategic Studies on Indonesia. He was the home affairs minister until 1993, and head of the armed forces before that. And he passed the ultimate test of Indonesian leadership: he won his spurs as a field general, putting down a rebellion in South Sulawesi.

When Rudini speaks of people being "cheated," he cannot be ignored. "Low-income people have been revolting against the state apparatus because they feel the state only sides with certain groups just to earn additional money," he recently told a conference that called for a total reform of Indonesia's political, economic, and judicial systems.

•　　•　　•

Opposition figures say this sort of push for reform from within the power elite is Indonesia's best hope for change. "There will never be a revolution in Indonesia," says a former Communist activist, now in his seventies, who spent more than a decade in jail after the 1965 civil war. "Not any more. Our time is gone. But there will be change. The embryonic conditions for freedom already exist," and they will need to be nurtured.

The Partai Komunis Indonesia (PKI) was an organized communist movement, with at least the sympathy if not the overt support of Sukarno. This time, there is no organized or widespread opposition. The PKI was banned and tens of thousands of its members murdered, precisely because they presented an alternative model of governance, says the activist. Most of them were Indonesians of Chinese heritage, descended from traders who first came to the archipelago centuries ago. "This time, the best we can hope for is a reform from the centre," says the activist, "perhaps behind Megawati."

•　　•　　•

Reform seems to be coming. Against all odds, the four-year-old human rights commission—set up with Canadian help and maintaining close ties with its Canadian counterpart—is focusing attention on the regime's excesses, especially the use of force to counter legitimate dissent. Recently, it called for an abolition of the country's subversion law, which threatens anyone who "endangers national stability" with the death penalty.

Beneath trellises clad with bougainvillaea, some of Indonesia's most prominent democrats gather at the outdoor Café Tempo on Forest Wood Road in East Jakarta to discuss what they are already calling the post-Suharto period. The café is named after a lively and at times brilliant newsmagazine that began as a clone of *Time*, but carried the weight and authority of *The Economist* by the time the government closed it.

It is the day after the Gadjah Mada demonstration. Earlier that Friday afternoon, the president abruptly cancelled a trip to Malaysia: a trip announced only days before to dispel rumours he is ill. Speculation is wild: Suharto is dead; he has had a stroke; he's so seriously ill the army and his daughter Siti Hardianti Rukmana have already stepped in to assume real power. The rumours reflect a sense that the end of Suharto is in sight. "In the history of Indonesia. It really doesn't matter whether he lasts two years or five years," says a clandestine democrat who is a prominent business executive by day.

Dissent is an act of bravery. Open dissent can be an act of folly. The business executive, and many others like him, dare not speak publicly. "If you quote me," says the executive; "it would be fatal."

At Café Tempo, the gathering of dissidents includes two of Indonesia's most courageous and independent thinkers, meeting for the first time in months. Arief Budiman is a political scientist whose democratic views led to his dismissal from his professorship at Satya Wacana (Spoken Truth), the leading Christian university in Indonesia. Now teaching at Melbourne University in Australia, he has just flown in. So has Goenawan Mohamad, who has been teaching in Japan. From 1971 to 1994, Goenawan was the editor and inspiration of *Tempo*. "It's a big chance for Indonesia to change," Budiman says of Suharto's faltering leadership, and the Indonesian economic crisis. "Whoever is in power has to comply with the International Monetary Fund and the World Bank." The economic restructuring imposed by the international agencies will also force the government to accommodate a broader debate on Indonesia's future, because no one in the government has new ideas or new ways forward. "These are processes in which the institution of democracy will become more established." Goenawan says "it's the most bitter irony the IMF has become a saviour in some form."

Indonesia, like China, has been a darling of international investors, who were all too willing to turn a blind eye to corruption and human rights abuses because "stable" governments delivered high growth and high profits. Now, says Goenawan, stability is in question: and it cannot be reestablished under any system of absolute power.

"The militarists can try to repress, but the World Bank will object," says Budiman. "The IMF and the World Bank want Indonesia to operate with transparency, reliable market mechanisms, and a clean and responsible government."

•   •   •

Goenawan feels the end of Suharto's rule will also bring into question the ability of the military to fulfil its constitutional function of providing social and political stability. Called *dwifungsi* or two functions, the role of social leadership is considered just as important as national defence for the armed forces. Suharto himself and many of his cabinet colleagues were generals or senior officers in the *Angkatan Bersenjatan Republik Indonesia* (Guardian Force of the Indonesian Republic, usually known by its acronym ABRI).

Suharto could not be in power without ABRI. And ABRI could not enjoy its role as the pre-eminent Indonesian institution without Suharto. Between ABRI and Suharto, opposition is tightly controlled and managed. There are no effective challenges to the established order.

Riots and street demonstrations, as Goenawan puts it, "indicate a growing rejection of the government's legitimacy," but there has been little in the way of an effective challenge to the New Order government.

Goenawan says ABRI "is overrated as an institution." In a country of two hundred million people, ABRI is a force of only five hundred thousand. It can keep public order to an extent, but it will be hard-pressed to enforce martial law in the absence of an absolute ruler like Suharto.

·   ·   ·

An Indonesian business executive who is a clandestine democrat says there are many people within ABRI with democratic sympathies, especially younger officers and rank-and-file soldiers who are "disgusted and horrified by the extent of the corruption." If they are ordered to use lethal force to put down widespread unrest in Java and Sumatra, he says, "the elite at the top can't count on their loyalty. These are soldiers who come from the people, they are not well paid, and they have to go and justify their actions in the villages, in the community. They will understand the hunger and the anger of their neighbours and their relatives. They will not kill their own."

After Suharto is gone, it will be harder for ABRI to stay united, says Goenawan. In the past, the common cause of independence was a binding force. But now, there's no longer an enemy, not even a political opposition capable of replacing the government. "There's no common enemy, no sparring partner to deal with," he says. "Fractions could happen so easily."

·   ·   ·

One such division began after Goenawan's magazine was shut down. *Tempo* was closed by the government on 21 June 1994, because it asked too many questions, uncovered too many scandals, and exposed the corruption within the government. *Tempo's* actions had the sympathy of some senior figures within ABRI, who thought the civilians in government were creating unrest with their arrogance and graft.

Led by then-information minister Harmoko, who is now speaker of the Indonesian parliament (and had become chairman of Golkar by the time Suharto eventually fell), the faction of technocrats within government muzzled *Tempo* to show no one, not even the most thoughtful, could criticize the government with impunity. (*Tempo* reopened in October 1998.) Its closure led to nationwide civil unrest, which Goenawan found "very moving and very encouraging."

It led young Indonesians to seriously question the legitimacy of the Suharto government: if the regime couldn't tolerate *Tempo*, would it listen to anyone? Some of those young Indonesians are in jail. Budiman Soedjatmiko, who spent many lunch hours at the Café Tempo on Forest Wood Road, is serving a fourteen-year jail sentence for provoking civil unrest. Muchtar Pakpahan, an independent labour leader who also frequented the café, remains on trial for his life on charges under the subversion laws. "There is no real government in Indonesia any longer," says the business executive who is a secret democrat. "There is no vision. These people continue in power by inertia, by sheer momentum. That's what's so frightening. Whoever steps in when the old man dies will come from a system that offers no real ideas and no original thoughts."

In a sense, everything in the country is on hold until the elections next March, say Canadian diplomats. They will either bring some sign of change, or leave today's dangerous inertia in place. "A lot will depend on the new vice-president and the new cabinet," says one diplomat. Suharto has chosen a different vice-president each term; under the Indonesian constitution, the vice-president would step in if the president were unable to continue. And the cabinet choice is important, says the Canadian diplomat "to see if some of the more corrupt people fall by the way side. The quality of the cabinet will really determine whether there is the political will to implement the economic recovery package, and to carry out necessary reforms."

Yet that seems too bloodless a view. There is foment in the air, a whiff of revolution in a country that has forgotten how to bring peaceful change. As twilight falls on Jakarta, as the ailing dictator leaves the country adrift, there is a feeling that the ultimate succession may be decided on the streets.

The last of Java's God-kings allows the sun to set

Jakarta, Indonesia, 23 May 1998

After thirty-two years, it was all over in a few words.

Outside, the clamour of Jakarta's protesters rent the air. Shuffling up to the microphone, the old man looked more like a grandfather than an iron-willed dictator, and to look at him one would not think he forged his country in battle and blood. Suharto, president of Indonesia, last of a line of Javanese God-kings spanning two millennia, was taking his leave. "For the assistance and support of the people while I led the nation and state of Indonesia, I express my thanks and I seek forgiveness if there were any mistakes and shortcomings."

On the surface of it, that was that. Yet nothing in the turbulent sprawl of Indonesia is what it first seems. Suharto's retirement, the ascent of B. J. Habibie to the presidency, the new "reform" cabinet that excludes Suharto's family and his most intimate friends, will end the chaos for now.

The first steps are encouraging. Late Friday, Justice Minister Muladi —who came to cabinet from the National Human Rights Commission —announced most political prisoners would be freed. High-profile captives like labour leader Muchtar Pakpahan and democracy activist Budiman Soedjatmiko should be eligible for the amnesty. And in an act unthinkable even weeks ago, Muslim leader Amien Rais went to Friday prayers at the al-Azhar mosque to announce he would stand for president when Habibie calls new elections.

The future of one of the world's most ancient and complex countries is far from predictable. The cheering multitudes in the streets, the young women handing flowers to soldiers, evoke the mood of the People Power revolution in the Philippines that toppled dictator Ferdinand Marcos a decade ago. Indeed, Habibie even spoke of "people power" in his inaugural speech, as he asked Indonesians to help him create a country "free from corruption, collusion and nepotism."

But Suharto is no Marcos, and Indonesia is far different from the Philippines. Habibie may have hit all the right notes in his speech, but saying it doesn't mean he's capable of doing it. Unlike Marcos, Suharto is not about to flee. Even though he has luxury homes outside Indonesia, even though he and his family have amassed a forty-billion dollar Canadian fortune during his rule, exile is not in the cards.

• • •

Modern, prosperous Indonesia—the country that existed until global currency speculators started attacking the Asian economic tigers last fall—was very much Suharto's creation. He is like a director who built the theatre, wrote the script, set the stage, hired the actors—he will not walk away until the last act is played out. Before he retired, he cast himself as a *pandito*—a sage to who people come for wisdom and advice. Having worked so long and hard to be seen as the saviour of Indonesia, Suharto does not want to leave his reputation—and his country—in ruins.

When Suharto came to power in 1965–66, six in ten Indonesians were too poor to feed themselves. By mid-1997, only one in twenty was mired in absolute poverty—unable to feed, clothe, and shelter themselves, unable to stave off hunger and malnutrition. By any objective measure, this was a mighty achievement in a country of 204 million people, the fourth most populous in the world. (By early 1999, it had mostly unravelled, the gains of thirty-four years abolished in less than eighteen months. Indonesia's fall was the most frightening plunge from riches to rags of any big country in the postwar world, even more cata-strophic than Russia's fall.)

Despite the corruption and cronyism Habibie promises to eliminate, Suharto's Indonesia was able to deliver a tangibly better life every year for most people. The price of that achievement—an absence of political freedom, a crushed opposition, and a ruling elite that put itself beyond challenge—was bearable so long as the economy flourished.

•　　•　　•

Even in the last decade of astonishing economic growth, discontent took root. The surge of the middle class left too many people behind. Despite improvements in the standard of living, the elite was skimming off far more than the country could sustain. One evening of decadence in one of Jakarta's many nightclubs could consume a teacher's monthly salary.

Suharto could not accept that anything was fundamentally wrong. His supporters would say that the family's income wasn't much different from what the chief executive of an Indonesia-sized corporation would amass legally. Suharto wasn't entirely wrong in blaming international speculators for dragging his economy down. The inescapable fact remains that during all the years of dictatorship, western countries and investors were only too willing to partner Suharto in developing—and exploiting—Indonesia.

Its internal connections between government and business were opaque as could be—no one knew where government ended and the private sector began, because in many instances the same players were involved in both. But for outsiders, Indonesia was a World Bank model of development. It enjoyed an economy with a fully convertible currency, free flows of capital, and open for foreign investment. Suharto played the capitalist game by big-business rules, and in exchange for access to Indonesia's riches, investors were only too glad to enrich the president, his cronies and other members of the ruling elite. Which makes it all the more ironic that Suharto's rule, a bulwark against communism, was at last brought down by capitalism.

The Indonesian economy was so free that the government had no means of knowing for sure how much money its private sector owed to international lenders. The finance ministry thought it was about twenty billion dollars U.S. To everyone's shock last summer, the real figure turned out to be sixty-eight billion dollars. Like Alberta during the boom, Indonesia's roaring economy commanded interest rates of up to 20 per cent—a handsome return for American and European banks which couldn't charge such rates back home.

Then came the currency shock, as a massive sell-off of currency by international speculators drove down the value of the Indonesian *rupiah*, the Thai *baht* and the Malaysian *ringgit* against the U.S. dollar. That left the Indonesian private sector stranded, unable to pay back dollar-denominated loans that cost a lot more in devalued currency.

•   •   •

By the reckoning of many economic analysts, Indonesia's problems were made worse by the International Monetary Fund's rescue package. Even though the Indonesian government had healthy finances, the IMF brought in the measures used to rescue bankrupt governments—slashed spending, higher interest rates, an end to subsidies.

Moreover, most of the IMF's actual cash investment went to paying off the foreign banks that lent money to Indonesia's private sector. In effect, the IMF covered the exposure of banks that should have borne the risks inherent in lending money at 19 and 20 per cent. While the IMF bailed out western banks, its harsh measures burst the bubble of prosperity for most ordinary Indonesians. As economic fortunes declined, they exposed the corrupt foundations of Suharto and the system he built. For one harsh truth of excessive private borrowing was this: business and politics are so intertwined, that it was hard to say where the government ended and private companies began: the ruling family and its friends owned so many private enterprises.

Every time they watched television, Indonesians enriched the first family and the networks they owned. The family pocketed the change from every toll road, profited from its department stores, took in cash every time an Indonesian smoked a pungent clove cigarette. The family's business monopolies were immense sources of cash. And any foreign investor who paid handsomely for a "partnership" with a first-family company was assured of success.

•　　•　　•

Before the crisis, there was a chance Suharto might retire. Yet he stood for an unprecedented seventh term as president in rubber-stamp elections last March, not least to salvage and preserve all he had built. Now, the salvage effort will continue from the sidelines. For all the flaws of Suharto's system, Indonesia faces a stark problem: it has no other. Any replacement will take time to build and evolve. For the moment, the interim leadership under Habibie will try to work with what it has. And the leader who comes after Habibie will need time too. Even if many Indonesians want a durable and democratic future, they will need the remnants of Suharto's system simply to keep the country going until a new one is launched.

That's why the army—which has a constitutional role to guarantee political and social stability—decided it was time for Suharto to step back and to begin the process of finding new leadership. The unthinkable alternative, for them, is a power vacuum that could lead to the disintegration of the country. That's a particular danger, because Indonesia is one of the largest and most diverse countries in the world. Rebellion is endemic. Conquered territories like East Timor still chafe at Jakarta's rule.

The archipelago is held together by a rigidly centralized government that equates power with control. A distance of 5500 kilometres separates the tip of Sumatra from Irian Jaya province's border with New Guinea. Within that span lie nearly 17,000 islands, dozens of cultures, more than one hundred languages and dialects, and nearly every strand of human history.

•   •   •

The volcanic landscape of Java has been a crossroads since the earliest human history. Pithecanthropus erectus—Java Man—once lived here. The Indonesian archipelago and the Indian subcontinent already enjoyed a vigorous exchange of trade and culture two thousand years ago. The China trade began between the third and fifth centuries A.D. By the thirteenth century, Islam arrived on the archipelago, spread by traders from western India. Over the centuries, it blended with the Buddhist-Hindu cultures of Sumatra and Java. The spice trade brought Europeans, starting in the fifteenth century. In 1602, Jan Pieterszoon Coen established a trade centre in what is now Jakarta, setting the stage for more than three centuries of Dutch control.

Dutch rule was particularly harsh. When the British temporarily controlled Java during the Napoleonic Wars, Sir Thomas Stamford Raffles was appalled at the hunger and suffering: far worse than in any British colony. Indonesian nationalism developed early this century, but the Dutch held on. Their grip was broken only after the Netherlands was overrun by Nazi Germany during the Second World War, and the Japanese occupied Indonesia. Astonishingly, the Dutch returned after the war to reclaim Indonesia. Amsterdam might have been a vanquished and hungry city, but there was an empire to be regained. The folly ended bitterly after much war and bloodshed, and the Indonesian republic, first proclaimed in 1945, at last became a reality in 1950.

Suharto was formed in that crucible. Like many young officers trained by the Dutch, he came under the spell of a charismatic nationalist leader called Sukarno, fought with him in the independence war, and served him loyally through the turbulent first years of Indonesia's freedom.

·   ·   ·

When Sukarno's mismanagement—a charismatic revolutionary is not necessarily a good manager—left Indonesia mired in poverty and corruption, Suharto led other generals in removing Sukarno from power. They claimed, in an allegation never proven, that there was the threat of a Communist coup against Sukarno, and they were moving in to save the republic. The key year was 1965. Sukarno, a gifted linguist who cast himself as both soldier-poet/philosopher-king and a Javanese mystic, foresaw a year of foment and change. Blending Indonesian and Latin, he called it *Tahun Vivere Pericoloso*—The Year of Living Dangerously.

Dangerous it was, for Sukarno, for leftists, for all who thought to take Indonesia in the socialist path. It was the height of anti-Communist fervour in the Vietnam War; the United States feared Southeast Asian countries would fall like dominoes, one after the other. In circumstances never really explained, half a dozen nationalist generals were assassinated—Sukarno supporters, one and all. An army faction led by Suharto immediately declared this the work of communist elements. Though it has never been clearly resolved, there is ample evidence that the assassinations were carried out by anti-Sukarno elements in order to justify a coup. The United States, grateful to have a staunch anti-Communist government in Indonesia, immediately gave its support to the plotters.

Tens of thousands of communists and suspected leftists—many of them ethnic Chinese—were murdered in late 1965 and early 1966. The government admits to half a million dead, unofficial estimate range as high as a million slain. The fear of that massacre, and a determination never to repeat it, still haunts Indonesia's leadership. It certainly stopped the military from supporting Suharto's rule with a show of brute force. Suharto's New Order government put communal harmony and consensus rule at the top of its Constitution. By definition, any move to break the consensus was seen as a traitorous act to be swiftly repressed—the opposition was sharply restricted.

Although political parties were limited, bodies with some political influence, if not power, were permitted. That's how Rais's Muhammadiyah Muslim movement was allowed to flourish. Religious associations are no substitute for actual governments. That's why the military and its leader General Wiranto—who heads the "new" cabinet Habibie announced— is still the key in the evolution of Indonesian politics. The power of the anti-Sukarno plotters should not be underestimated. One of the first to turn against Sukarno in 1965, for instance, was a young journalist named Harmoko. He grew up to become the minister of information who banned the newsmagazine *Tempo*, later became Speaker of the Parliament and chair of the ruling party Golkar. And in the second *Tahun Vivere Pericoloso*, 1998, he was the first of the senior rulers to tell Suharto it was time to step aside.

•　　•　　•

This elite is nothing if pragmatic. They will do what is necessary to survive. If that means democracy, so be it—so long as it is under their control. Even if they want to embrace a more open democracy—and many military officers do—they want to move slowly and gradually. Wiranto, who is only fifty-one, has the patience to look beyond Habibie. And he has been astute enough to know he cannot openly seize power, and expect his leadership to be widely accepted. Habibie clearly is a short-term figure. After Suharto, Wiranto and the others with real power look ahead; they may seek a figurehead who will put an acceptable face on the leadership while Indonesia embarks on political and economic reforms. That face is unlikely to belong to the opposition's Rais, or any of Suharto's coteries. The unifying figure might well be opposition leader Megawati Sukarnoputri, Sukarno's daughter, who sat on the sidelines as Rais joined the protesters who toppled Suharto. Megawati (her Sanskrit name means The Light of the Clouds) was leader of the opposition Indonesian Democratic Party, until she was ousted in July 1996 by a government-engineered coup.

The riots that followed—and were quickly quelled—foreshadowed the unrest that brought Suharto down. Megawati has what Rais and Suharto's entourage lack—Sukarno's blood. In the Javanese mysticism that lies a scratch below the veneer of modernity, this means she carries her father's God-given power within her. A ruler's *teja*, or divine energy, is passed on through blood. It will be taken as an article of faith by millions of Indonesians (as was shown in immense pro-Megawati rallies at the end of 1998) that Megawati carries her father's spirit and soul within her. And the Sukarno name is still magic in Indonesia, as time erases memories of his misrule.

Megawati refused to join Habibie's reform cabinet, but she may well be tempted to stand for president with military backing. Indonesia needs someone who will earn the people's goodwill and grace as it rebuilds its economy and moves towards democracy.

Right now, she seems to be Suharto's best bet, as the patriarch attempts to salvage his imploding kingdom.

The longest night's uncertain dawn

Jakarta and Yogyakarta, Indonesia, 24 May 1998

Not jubilation, not anger, just an overwhelming sense of relief. When news of Suharto's resignation came late Wednesday, my first thought was of my Indonesian friends. By stepping back to wield power behind the scenes, Suharto spared his country another bloodbath. I thought of my friend A, his wife R and their baby N in their Jakarta suburb. He is ethnic Chinese, she is Javanese; they see themselves as Indonesian. But that's not how some of the rioting mobs saw A and others with similar facial features. As so often happens, the ethnic Chinese became the scapegoats. Their shops were looted; their homes were burned. Perhaps now, the end of Suharto buys them some time, if not peace.

I thought of my friend M in Yogyakarta, who might have been reporting on a 250,000-strong rally in the ancient Javanese capital. She works in Suharto's hometown, but when I last saw her at the end of 1996 she spoke openly about the emerging discontent against the patriarch. In 1992, she had been a believer. Suharto's regime might have been corrupt, but it had done good things. Yet at our last dinner, the balance shifted: the extent of the first family's greed was appalling, and M began to wonder how long they could carry on.

Suharto's money-skimming ways, the fat contracts and monopolies awarded to the children, made them among the richest people on the planet. And even in his hometown, there were rumblings of discontent. They would gather force throughout the spring of 1998. The anti-Suharto revolt began in Yogyakarta—even the hometown crowd had enough.

It all appeared so different in March 1992, when M took me to a modest village outside Yogyakarta. The landscape was magical. Ricefields of a green so vivid they hurt the eye, a sky of shifting cloudscapes, and dominating all, the smoking cone of the enormous Merapi volcano. It was like stepping into a medieval world, with few signs of modernity. Mystery and magic and the volcano guided the world; peasant existence was much as it always had been. The only difference between past centuries and this were the basics of industrial civilization: electricity, paved roads, and automobiles. We pulled onto a side road, passed orchards, more ricefields, and the jeep came to a stop. M waved with a flourish: "This is where the president's family lived." The moment I saw Suharto's village house, time and distance fell away: it might have been a part of my grandparents' village, right down to the chickens, the giant mango trees, and the hanging roots of the spreading banyan trees. I knew the architecture all too well from my own village childhood in India. From the outside, you see a couple of long, low wings of adjacent rooms, earthen walls, and thatched roofs, a covered veranda running in front.

In Central Java, the walls were strips of latticed bamboo. These days, evidence of Indonesia's growing prosperity, there are many more tiled roofs than thatch. And more often than not, the walls are brick and plaster. In eastern India, one of the wings might front onto the village's main street. You'd climb a couple of steps to the veranda, then into one of the rooms. And if you were actually invited in, you'd leave the room by another door, giving on to an inner courtyard—the real heart of a village home.

This was the typical home for joint families well into this century— several generations living under one set of roofs, with a nominal separation, if any, between the households sharing the same complex. It was a community within a community, the pattern of human settlement and development in many parts of Asia for the greater part of the millennium—before the development of urban centres and an educated middle class took children off the land.

Suharto's ancestral home was set off the street around an unpaved outer courtyard. There appeared to be no one around: there was nothing to either encourage or discourage casual visitors. We had a look and left. Within a few minutes we passed a huge building rising out of the paddies: Bangsa Manggala, an agricultural university bequeathed by Suharto to his home region. It was this sort of "generosity" that kept people faithful. Universities, decent health care, better food: all the bounty to be expected of a Javanese God-king. And of course, no one should be impolite enough to dissent.

Full bellies and captive minds might have been enough, once upon a time, but the modern world is catching up very fast with medieval Indonesia. Even a God-king can seem no better than a common thief, once the magic fades.

Indonesia enjoys the novelty of truth

Yogyakarta, Indonesia, 23 August 1998

"What do you see in the sea?" B asked, finally breaking a long and companionable silence. Until B spoke, there had been only the sound of the wind washing over the bluffs and the long rollers of the Java Sea breaking far below. It was our first chance to speak in true privacy, when I met him on an autumn day five years ago. On the southern coast of Java, one of the most densely populated islands of the world, we had found a spot away from the crowds on the nearby public beach. B didn't really expect an answer. Like me, B gazed across the infinity of water, an uninterrupted expanse sweeping all the way down to Antarctica. Here, alone before the sea, it was at last a time to speak of truth—a rare commodity in Indonesia during the Suharto dictatorship.

B taught literature at one of Indonesia's leading universities—even with the current climate of reform, I cannot risk divulging B's full identity—and tried to give students what autocracies fear most: the power of critical thought. Even alone, B spoke in a way that could pass a censor's scrutiny—no matter how much B wanted to trust me; this was the simplest precaution. "My students enjoy Ionesco," B ventured, referring to Romanian dramatist Eugene Ionesco, who illuminates absurdity. "It helps them to understand their country." That act of defiance by B and some of B's colleagues, turning out students who could think independently about their life and their society, may finally be ready to bear fruit.

Since Suharto's decision to step aside in May, truth is rising from its deathbed—and with the truth come the first stirrings of genuine freedom. For the first time, the full and terrible story of the May riots is coming to light. In the charged atmosphere of Suharto's last days, the world's eyes were on the shooting of middle-class students at Trisakti University, and the riots directed principally against ethnic-Chinese businesses. Now the deeper truths emerge—with the riots came rape and murder. Systemic, organized rapes of ethnic Chinese—carefully documented by Jesuit priest Sandyawan Sumardi and a nationwide network of volunteers calling themselves "*Untuk Kemanusiaan*"—For Humanity. Through persistence and compassion, they have documented details of 152 rapes— some of which culminated in murder—during the intense days of rioting May 13–15. Typically, a band of looters would destroy a shop, rape the women, and sometimes throw them into the blazing ruins.

This truth has been difficult to gather, in part because the shame of the victims prevents many from coming forward.

But the other chilling aspect is how uncomfortable Indonesia's powerful are in confronting the truth. A senior military commander this week warned human rights groups not to "exaggerate" tales of rape. And as Father Sumardi writes in his report, his volunteers "many times get warnings not to continue their activities even in this supposed-to-be reformation spirit, speaking about and listening sympathetically to the victims of the rapes is still considered a threat [to the state-nation? Or to some official elements?]."

There are other truths emerging to answer Sumardi's parenthetical questions—the first being that in the minds of the Suharto-era regime, there was no difference between the nation and "some official elements."

Suharto's son-in-law, Major-General Prabowo Subianto, has taken personal responsibility in the kidnapping and disappearance of political opponents earlier this year. He says he "misinterpreted" the orders of his superior officers. There were three such superiors it turns out, including Suharto.

Such confession may not be quite on the scale of South Africa's truth commission, but it's a start. So is the acknowledgement that Xanana Gusmao, jailed leader of the East Timor independence movement, is not a terrorist but a political prisoner. Gusmao held a press conference at Cipinang prison to demand the unconditional release of all political detainees. The story isn't what he said, but that he was allowed to say it.

The difficulty of embracing truth, after decades of living in shadows and lies, is vividly illustrated in Indonesia's first modern political opinion poll—a sampling of five thousand by the University of Indonesia. Six in ten respondents either refused to say how they would vote, said they wouldn't vote, or claimed not to know whom they would support. Of those who answered, fewer than 13 per cent of respondents favoured President B. J. Habibie's Golkar party, which ruled Indonesia throughout the Suharto era, while 40 per cent chose Megawati Sukarnoputri, daughter of the president Suharto toppled to gain power.

These are small steps, small beginnings. Yet the truth, no matter how difficult it may turn out to be, is the strongest foundation of a civil society. People like B, and those who learned from B, have a special obligation to become guardians of truth. They are part of Indonesia's emergence from darkness.

How the borderless world came to be born

Cambridge, London, and Liverpool, England, January to April 1987

Some of the by-products of the global economy—tribalism, racial tension, displacement, joblessness, a gap between rich and poor—were not particularly evident so long as the global boom of the 1990s came along. Yet before that boom, the emerging and still unresolved problems of globalization were becoming evident in Margaret Thatcher's Britain. I was there. This second memoir drawn from that time bears witness how to the borderless world emerged from what was once the planet's mightiest empire.

What is the real England? What are its faces? I had glimpsed some of them already. On the bus from Cambridge to London one day, I made a jarring transition from the pastoral essence of England to a study in urban melancholy: the East End of London. From the bus I looked at a group of children in school uniform, no older than twelve or thirteen, walking down the street. They had fresh faces and looked as happy as all kids do when they're out of school. They turned to cross the street. One of them caught my eye and mouthed: "F— off you Paki."

I was surprised and sad. I had heard and read about racial problems here and there, but dismissed them as aberrations, caused as much by poverty, economic disparity, and a sense of hopelessness as anything. But to see such casual hatred in a twelve-year-old, to see that child's face twist into a bestial expression, dispirited me deeply. If it has come to the point where the mere sight of a brown face will trigger such a violent emotion, I thought, something has gone terribly wrong.

A few days later, John Pilger wrote in the *Independent* about a girl named Nasreen, whose family had been the victim of appalling tribal attacks—their storefront smashed, excrement put through the mailbox, the police powerless to stop it. Nasreen wrote to Thatcher, whose values of hard work and self-reliance the family embraced. They ascribed to neo-Victorian values of thrift and perseverance. How then to escape the nightmare of gangs of indolent and violent youth who forced the family to barricade themselves? Nasreen got a reply from someone at the home ministry who was sorry he could not be more helpful, and suggested the family keep on calling the police, even though they didn't come. An Englishman's home may once have been his castle, but in this case it had become a fortress. Nasreen, with her cockney accent, had been in contact with Pilger for three years before he wrote this particular account. He called her "Anne Frank with a telephone."

Pilger accused the police of racism. I put this to two policemen who were at Wolfson as part of a management course. One had grown up in the East End of London. "It's a tough part of town," said Bob. "That's just the way things are there." It was understandable why some people thought the police racist, or at least tribal, in their behaviour. A police inspector was on trial for wounding a black woman left paralyzed after the shooting. Court heard the man describe how he was tense, because he thought he was to confront a suspected armed robber: he said he just shot at the first thing he saw. The police officer was acquitted, and the victim said she felt no bitterness. But neighbours, and others in the community, thought the police had used weapons because they knew they were going into a black neighbourhood, and presumed guilt on the part of the suspects.

•　　•　　•

Such tribalism existed on both "sides." A trial heard how a police officer had been slashed and hacked to death by a mob during a riot: multiple slashes, his jaw opened up, the head severed, and his colleagues powerless to help. The riot itself was a sorry example of tribalism. It occurred in December 1985, in a housing estate in the North London district of Tottenham. During the course of a police raid, a black woman suffered a heart attack and died. Within hours, shielded riot police were facing a mob armed with machetes and petrol bombs. The ringleader of the men convicted of murdering the policeman was on bail at the time of the attack: he had been charged in an earlier murder. The trial judge criticised the police handling of the case: three juveniles were acquitted, and the judge said they were the victims of police "oppression." One 13-year-old boy had been interrogated for hours, wearing only his under-wear and a blanket. He had told the police anything they suggested to him. Neither he nor the other juveniles had been given access to legal counsel; none had been told they had the right to remain silent. Such breakdown in police procedure, like the shock of a raid that produces a heart attack, could only be due to visceral, tribal responses on the part of both the police and the people whose safety and welfare they were sup-posed to assure.

Racism was not the only tribal confrontation evident in England. There were ugly scenes on television of Fortress Wapping: it was a year since Rupert Murdoch broke the back of the feather-bedded Fleet Street press unions, moving his newspaper operations to a heavily guarded establishment in London's reborn docklands, staffed by a new brand of unions. Ever since, there had been confrontation and daily picketing, and a climate of bitterness amounting to warfare. Around the anniversary of the move, there was an altercation outside the Wapping gates: hand-to-hand combat between the crowd and the police. The graphic images brought to mind European history, peasants trying to storm the feudal manor, only to be repelled by guards. If Murdoch represented the hard face of capitalism, then the unions represented the lengths to which people will go when they perceive their very survival is at stake. Shortly after that defining riot, the union gave up. Fleet Street had moved from an archaic mode of production into the twenty-first century, but at what human cost? What had happened to civility? To consensus? To negotiating in good faith? Or had it, in this case, come down to a tribal clash between two groups fighting for survival?

．　　　．　　　．

The racism I thought I had seen, not xenophobia so much as a tribal sense of hatred, was it so deep a current it could not be overcome? The *Guardian* ran ads for race-relations officers, who would help to build bridges between minorities and the larger community. Such people were offered salaries of some nineteen thousand pounds a year, more than twice the bottom range for the deputy head of an elementary school, roughly what my academic supervisor David Fieldhouse earned in his pre-retirement position as the Vere Harmsworth Professor of Imperial and Naval History and Fellow of Jesus College at Cambridge University. It occurred to me that the long-term solutions to tribal racism: changing social attitudes, promoting understanding, ought to begin at the school level. By apparently underpaying teachers, thereby deterring motivated people from teaching, what social objectives were being achieved? Did it do any good to appoint well-qualified people to improve race relations after the problem had already gotten out of hand? How much could a race relation unit do if attitudes formed early and hardened to the point where a twelve-year-old could muster con-centrated hate?

The symbols of racism were being fought, rather than racism itself, to the point of drowning out voices of reason. A handicapped child who had learned "Baa Baa Black Sheep" as his first nursery rhyme was told this was not acceptable: The council of Islington, a London borough, had deemed it a racist rhyme. They had a racism adviser for preschoolers. How absurd, I thought. What is this but the most nonsensical devotion to symbolism, the sort of tribal arrogance that deliberately seeks offence where none is intended? Because the "black sheep" produced wool for its master in the rhyme, it was supposed to be a racist connotation? Was there some link with slavery I missed? Who were these humourless guffins bound on revising nursery rhymes? And how would they revise the English language next? Would a White Christmas be offensive to them? Should magic no longer be referred to as the black arts? Should white coffee and black coffee be referred to as coffee with and without milk? Would the mere mention of colour in any context breed offence? It reminded me of the zealotry of the newly converted, oblivious to any ideas outside the received wisdom of their new faith: or was it again a tribal reaction, born of a collective insecurity?

•   •   •

I spent time in London with old family friends. Prafulla was an artist who had recently gained renown for publishing a book called *Through Brown Eyes*, about his personal experience of discrimination in England. Derek, his long-time companion, was a lawyer. In that bitter winter of 1987, Derek would tell me of the homes he visited in the course of his work with the rent control tribunal: homes where old people could afford to heat only one room, and even then, it was clear they had turned the heat on to accommodate the visitor. Bedroom, living room, dining room, parlour, all centred on a rationed fire. Every other room would be damp and clammy, Derek said, and the people wore layers of sweaters and coats. Outside, a few centimetres of snow had thrown the country into chaos. There were many debates in the House of Commons about a five-pound payment to freezing pensioners: the government had some sort of formula for the temperatures at which the payments for heating would begin. An earnest minister explained how a new brochure would explain all this. How typical, I thought. Instead of handing out a payment, print a brochure explaining how to get one.

Finally, the government decided to come through with emergency payments, regardless of temperature. What a fuss over a relatively paltry sum, I thought. Would there have been such a fuss if the government hadn't sold off state-owned British Gas to the private sector? A Cambridge sociologist told me the gas rates had risen just before privatization, simply to make the company more attractive. Now that pensioners were stung by the high rates, the government drummed up a rebate.

•   •   •

Outside Harrods, I bought a bag of roast chestnuts for fifty pence from a street vendor. Inside were dresses selling for four hundred pounds and more—were they really worth eight hundred bags of chestnuts? A teacher making 7,500 pounds a year would be nothing more than a visitor: like the poor of yesteryear the middle class would glue their noses to the Harrod's shop-window, even though they may be better educated than the newly rich who shopped there. Surely, I thought, this would only make the gap between desire and attainment all the deeper. It was a refrain I heard from many middle-class people, when they told me: "I couldn't afford to buy the home I'm in if I had to buy at today's prices." Here too was the thread of displacement running through England's social fabric. Harrods dresses and affordable houses were just a part of it. But the displacement spread from the ever-poorer middle class, and afflicted those least able to resist, the ones without economic power in a society where wealth was increasingly the only measure of human worth.

In Fulham, a middle- and working class neighbourhood across from fashionable Chelsea, simple homes were being turned into fashionable "cottages" and sold for a fortune. This was no more than simple market economics, but it killed communities as long-term residents moved out, and inner city was "reclaimed." Once these people at the lowest end of the economic scale were displaced, where could they go? Peter, another police officer taking the Wolfson course, told me that this sense of displacement was a major factor in the riots that swept Britain's inner cities in the early 1980s.

Peter is an unusually sensitive police officer, extremely bright, with few illusions about the government he serves. A detective-inspector in the Metropolitan Police, he worried about the future of the displaced and the effects of tribalism. He saw the new attitudes towards wealth robbing many Britons of a meaningful life. He despaired about the long-term unemployed, those who can never hope to find a permanent job without substantial retraining. He wondered where displacement and despair would lead. Peter's worst fear was the rise of a criminal class such as prevailed in Victorian times, at the height of Empire: in a society where naked wealth is paraded, where the economic disparity is evident from neighbourhood to neighbourhood, why wouldn't the permanently disadvantaged turn to crime?

Peter and I agreed the decline in the industrial economy, the continued long-term unemployment, the emphasis on the service sector of the economy, would ultimately lead to a revival of a servant class for the newly rich—not as actual household servants, perhaps, but as piece-rate workers catering the ancillary needs of people who had more money than they could reasonably spend. Thatcher's government fudged the jobless numbers by counting people in short-term training as fully employed, but the state was carrying four million unemployed people. Their jobs had moved away forever, to jurisdictions with lower costs, their skills no longer in demand.

•   •   •

An election was coming sometime in 1987, and the political manoeuvring was well under way. Labour appeared to have committed political suicide by advocating unilateral nuclear disarmament, leading the mass-market newspapers to declare the opposition was running up "the white flag of surrender" to the nuclear-armed Soviet Union. In the absence of any prospect of opposition victory, the field was left open to Prime Minister Thatcher and her cabinet to reshape Britain any way they saw fit.

The overriding economic problem remained unemployment. Thatcher's senior minister Norman Tebbit had become celebrated for his observation that in his day, when his father didn't have work, he simply got on his bicycle and moved to an area where he could find a job. Despite Tebbit's fond belief that every poor boy could become rich through effort alone—a theory disproved by the relatively small number of millionaires among the population at large—this was more easily said than done. The main barrier to labour mobility was the widening gap between the poor north and the booming Southeast. A weekend television special told of a man who had followed Tebbit's advice. After years of unemployment and part-time work, he had moved to London to take a job as a bus conductor.

He was delighted to work. But what had it done to his life? Housing costs in London were such that he could not afford to bring his family. He had to send money home for their upkeep. In London, he could afford only one small room in a house. He would return to this every night after a shift on the bus, standing up for the entire time. For him, it was a cup of tea, a bite to eat, and straight to bed. He missed his wife and children. It was too much trouble to come home from a tiring day and cook supper for one alone—besides, the cooking facilities had to be shared. He could get home every other weekend, but only if he hitch-hiked. The cost of a bus ticket was beyond his income. He had the choice of returning to his family, and forty-five pounds a week dole, or remaining separated from his loved ones—leading a bleak and rigorous life simply to have the dignity of work rather than enduring the stigma of being unemployed. The man was thinking of giving up his job—he found it unbearable to be away from home.

At least he had tried to move. For those with homes in the north, getting decent housing in the Southeast was impossible. A three-bedroom detached house in Preston, a comfortable city north of Liverpool and a former cotton-spinning centre, cost less than forty thousand pounds. Similar accommodation in an equivalent London neighbourhood like Richmond cost three hundred thousand pounds. Rental properties were scarce and costly. A landlord let his flats sit idle rather than rent them for 150 pounds a week because that gave him hardly any return on his investment, "only five per cent return, less than I could get" from almost anything else. He didn't charge more because he thought no one would pay.

•　　•　　•

A friend from Canada moved to a world-economy job in London at a salary of twenty-seven thousand pounds, working for Inmarsat, the international maritime satellite communications service. This was regal income by English standards. He could afford a small two-bedroom flat in an attractive area only because his company paid a rent subsidy. His accommodation in Hampstead cost two hundred pounds a week—even with the subsidy; the rent stretched his means. How far could a man who "got on his bicycle" expect to go in such a property market?

He would have little choice but to share the bus conductor's fate, to rent a room in a house. Such a rental could typically run to seventy-five pounds a week. It would afford little privacy, unless he wished to stay shut in his room. Family accommodation would be out of the question. Set against an average industrial salary of 169 pounds a week, a rent of 75 pounds a week would leave little room for discretionary spending. Misguided government policy had brought about the lack of suitable rental accommodation. By allowing homeowners to write off their mortgage interest against income tax, the state in effect told people to buy homes rather than rent them.

By limiting the choice and effectively penalizing people who chose not to own homes, the government gave developers little incentive to invest in rental accommodation. Worse, much of the available housing was governed by rent controls, which simply meant controlled housing offered the landlord too little incentive to upgrade or renovate deteriorating housing; and uncontrolled housing was far too expensive for the working person to afford. It seemed to me ending tax relief for mortgages, and removing rent controls would give people the choice between renting and buying; it would allow supply and demand to determine a fair allocation of rental accommodation.

Poor people need not be condemned to artificially high housing costs: rather than keeping rents down, the government should offer subsidies to individuals so they could afford higher rents. By offering subventions to needy people rather than removing the incentive for landlords to offer better housing, the quality and quantity of rental housing would improve. This in turn would enable much greater labour mobility between depressed and booming areas of the economy. The poor quality of much of the state-owned housing was eroding the health of many working class Britons and adding to the state's already high health-care bill. According to a report called "The Health Divide," released by a government-created body called the Health Education Council, the gap between rich and poor is increasingly reflected in the health of Britons.

"Whether social position is measured by occupational class, or by assets such as house and car ownership, or by employment status, a similar picture emerges," wrote researcher Margaret Whitehead. "Those at the bottom of the social scale have much higher death rates than those at the top. This applies at every stage of life. All the major killer diseases now affect the poor more than the rich and so do most of the less common ones. The less favoured occupational classes also experience higher rates of chronic sickness and their children tend to have lower birth weight, shorter stature and other indicators suggesting poor health status. The unemployed and their families have considerably worse physical and mental health than those in work. Until recently, direct evidence unemployment caused this was not available. Now there is substantial evidence of unemployment causing a deterioration in mental health with improvement observed on reoccupation."

•   •   •

The untreated mentally ill were much in evidence. In London and Cambridge, people wandered the streets speaking to themselves or shouting at passers-by. Some slept in subway cars, slugging beer on the District line. Standards of health care were changing. Private insurance was allowed to compete with the National Health Service. Those who could afford to pay received much better medical treatment than working Britons.

They didn't have to wait in queue. Some health authorities were told health care costs were rising "too fast" because doctors were seeing "too many" patients. The proposed solution was to reduce the number of consultations and hospital beds so fewer people would be treated. Doctors thought this absurd. But health authorities were told that unless they cut budgets by treating fewer patients, they would be replaced. It appeared obvious to all but government that economic deprivation only increased the demand on health services. In order to achieve a healthier population—surely the most effective way of cutting costs—people would need security and stability in their lives, and nutritional counselling to change eating habits that produced some of the highest instances of preventable coronary disease in the world. Treating fewer patients, leaving larger numbers of the sick uncared for, did not seem an agreeable solution. I thanked my good fortune no Canadian had to face such a dreadful choice. Ignoring the sick would not make them go away. And who would measure the long-term social cost of illnesses left untreated?

•   •   •

Poverty and unemployment only deepened the gap between the rich and all the rest in the Thatcher years. The number of English children living in "extreme" poverty was estimated at four hundred thousand in 1983. Nearly 150,000 children were homeless, in a country that was damp and chilly for much of the year. Politicians did not seem to understand a healthy population is a more productive one. The report recommended higher allowances for families with children and better maternity benefits. It said there should be free school meals for all. It urged better housing and working conditions. All of these things, presumably, would lead to a healthier society. Government evaluated the recommendations, said they would cost two thousand million pounds, and rejected that expenditure. This appeared extremely shortsighted to me. Investing two billion pounds might save millions of pounds in future social costs. The Chancellor of the Exchequer even had a budget surplus to play with. He used part of that to reduce Britain's relatively high personal income tax rate from twenty-nine pence on the pound, and the rest in modest public investments. But if the Tories had summoned the political will to explain two billion pounds needed to be spent on a healthier society in order to provide a better life for more Britons, and to reduce the costs of the welfare state in the long run, who would have balked at such an investment?

The refusal to invest in health, the problems of mass unemployment in bypassed economies like Northern England's industrial belt, made me wonder how much thought politicians had given to their nation's security. They were willing to spend billions of pounds on nuclear systems or conventional arms to guard their country from external attack, but appeared ignorant of the serious internal divisions developing within Britain. Surely security in the broadest sense included a vigorous and stable society that could be happy and productive? What Britain needed, I thought, were a new definition of security and a new approach to employment. If social stability were considered an essential for national security, then it made sense to invest in programmes that would enable every Briton to live a healthy and secure life. From such a climate, economic growth and efficiency would emerge. If obvious disparities broadened, if there were large numbers of idle people without any hope of a productive future, there would be social unrest, perhaps a repeat of the inner city riots that had swept England in the early 1980s.

•　　•　　•

One evening in Cambridge I sat at dinner with a clever woman who taught at Portsmouth. In fact, both she and her husband were teachers, but they saved and sacrificed in order to send their school-aged child to a private school. It's not that the calibre of teachers is better in a private school, she said, but public education is in a shambles. Public school teachers are leaping to private schools. "We tell student teachers they'd be crazy to enter the profession."

Because hers was a two-income family, she was able to provide a decent education for her child. She and her husband, entrusted with giving England a qualified and motivated generation of graduates to keep their country competitive in the global marketplace, could not guarantee such an education for the children they taught. It had little to do with them, everything to do with the Thatcher government's commitment to quality public education.

If England didn't invest heavily in education, where would it expect to be in a rapidly changing world economy? By the early 1980s, it already was evident that the world's economic impetus had shifted to

Asia, and that Asia, with its burgeoning industrial economies, enormous pools of labour, and potentially huge consumer markets, would be the engine of the world economy for decades to come. Traditional manufacturing industries in the West were in decline. Western industrial countries were moving from an industrial economy to a technological one, based more on the provision of services and ideas than on goods. The countries that would be most successful in the next century would be the ones most able to live by their wits, to successfully tailor their economic behaviour to the demands of the new frontier in Asia.

Was it a mere policy oversight, or was it something deeper, something rooted in the psyche of Britain's leaders, that made them overlook the fact that their former colonies might one day be the masters of Britain's economic destiny? Was it the pride of the aristocrat fallen on hard times who refused to accept a helping hand from his former servant? Was it good enough for Mrs. Thatcher to simply say spending on research and development are at record levels, when budget cuts at universities forced the closure of entire departments, and the permanent loss of talented staff to other countries? Low English salaries were already driving talented minds away. Everyone fretted about the brain drain, yet there appeared little incentive to stay. At universities affected by cuts, broad programs in liberal arts were being sacrificed for ones with "practical" applications in science and technology. This was a time when companies in North America were coming to value people with broad education and analytical minds, recognizing that a worker may have to be retrained five or six times in a career. Of the insular trends I had seen, this shortsightedness in education seemed more dangerous to me than the strands of poverty and racism: education was the answer, yet it was most in peril.

Was the displacement of English people, the evolution of an impoverished north and a prosperous south any less calamitous a change than the partition of the Indian subcontinent? Was the polarity between rich and poor, the imminent impoverishment of the middle class, any less turbulent a social transition? The change brought the death of hope among good people, the death of ways of life no longer valued in a wealth-oriented system, a ruling ideology that reduced human beings to commodities—measuring human lives by productive capacity, as a grocer might grade fruit.

A postscript, February 1999

In the Thatcher years, boundaries were being drawn everywhere, even as the power of economics was erasing traditional boundaries and divisions. The free-market capitalism unleashed by the prime minister was the foundation of what came to be known as neo-liberal economics. What I saw in 1987 foreshadowed the rest of the century: economics erasing boundaries, cultures and societies trying to erect new ones. I did not know it then, but I was experiencing the birth pangs of the borderless world.

The Euro does what conquerors could not

Paris and Tain l'Hermitage, France, 26 April 1998

As she does every Sunday, Marthe Camauzet comes to the neighbourhood shops in the Place Maubert for her holiday provisions before going to church. The stylishly dressed retiree's melodious "bonjour!" is more sung than spoken, as she pops into the baker, the greengrocer, the fishmonger, and the creamery. In the poultry shop, she inspects a free-range farm chicken at nine dollars a kilogram and a certified Bresse chicken, one of France's great delicacies, at nearly twice the price. She won't even look at the mass-produced chicken—the kind sold in Canadian supermarkets—at $3.50 a kilogram. "Industrial meat, how do you know where it comes from?" She settles on the farm chicken because she takes pride in being a smart consumer. "I can always know a fair price."

Come January 1, she'll need to learn a new set of prices. Alongside the familiar francs, everything will be priced in a brand new currency. On May 2 and 3, while Camauzet makes her rounds at the Place Maubert, the European Community will gather in Brussels to launch the global economy's newest superpower—a union of 360 million people forming the largest economy in the world.

The leaders will choose the first nations to use the common European currency, called the Euro. They will make the national economies of eleven European countries into one: using a single currency guided by one central bank, with a free flow of people, workers, products, and services. The North American equivalent would be replacing the U.S. dollar, the Canadian dollar and the peso with a single currency, making all three countries give up their economic independence to a larger North American union, and forcing all three to coordinate their budgets and their economic and trade policies.

European leaders hope that such a large, integrated economy will be much better able to weather recessions. They believe stable, coordinated and prudent economic policies will lead to steady growth and a steady decline in unemployment. Camauzet will have to adjust quickly to the new pricing—by 2002, the French franc will be gone altogether. All prices will be in Euros, in France and at least ten other countries in the European Monetary Union. "It might be challenging at first, but not really so difficult if truth be told," says Camauzet. "I'm sure we'll work it out together," she says, indicating the shopkeepers. For Camauzet and her generation, who were children or teenagers during the Second World War, the introduction of the Euro on 1 January 1999, will cap a remarkable historical evolution. Countries that were enemies in humankind's bloodiest war will form the nucleus of an economically united Europe.

The union is much more than a free-trade area, because the member countries will merge their economies and be directed by one central bank. Countries can still set their own budgets and collect their own taxes, but they'll be forced to coordinate their economic policy to keep inflation, interest rates, and budget deficits within legislated limits. In practice, it means individual countries can't offer business subsidies or increase social spending unless they stay within the common budget guidelines. Member nations will also lose another major freedom: the ability to devalue their currency to make their exports more competitive. For instance, Italy can't lower the value of the lira to make Fiat cars cheaper for French and German buyers. Once everything is priced in Euros, any changes in value of the Euro will be decided by the central bank.

The common currency is the latest step in the Europe envisioned in the aftermath of the Second World War. Since the first European Economic Community was launched under French leadership forty-one years ago, French governments of every political hue pushed the notion of a united Europe as the guarantor of peace and prosperity. Now, with a common currency, most of Western Europe will become one nation—at least in economic terms. "It's one of the most important events of the century," says Richard Bastien, a senior Canadian diplomat based at the embassy in Paris. It will "tie the economic destinies of the member countries more closely than at any time since the Roman Empire." For Bastien, the advent of the Euro has "striking parallels" with the evolution of Canadian federalism. By creating a single currency and a single economy, Europe is "establishing a de facto federation." If Canada were a purely economic union, the need to coordinate common economic policy would demand shared political decisions, says Bastien. The European common currency "raises a fundamental question: can one have a common monetary policy, less room to manoeuvre on budgets, and harmonized fiscal policies without adopting common social policies?"

So far, Europeans are staying away from defining a formal political union—French officials say it will be challenging enough to advance the economic merger. And it may not be practical given the minefield of European history. But the merger of economic power, and the loss of budget-making independence, will have the effect of a political union. "Currency, which for centuries reinforced a national identity, will now reinforce a European identity," says Bastien. And given the rules set for the Euro, member countries will be "more constrained than Canadian provinces" in setting economic policy.

It is too early to say how the Euro will affect Canada. Since we're part of a large trading bloc—the North American Free Trade area—it will mean more streamlined global trade. But it will also mean more competition, as united Europe becomes a single market fighting for investment, exports and jobs with a North American economy that isn't nearly as integrated. "People have no idea of the overwhelming change that's coming in their lives," says banker Christine Grange, who works in the French provinces where the impact will be most keenly felt. "Nothing will stay the same."

Grange is in international financing in the Rhone valley city of Valence, six hundred kilometres south of Paris. Once a quiet cousin to the sprawling city of Lyon ninety-five kilometres away, Valence has seen its population nearly double to one hundred thousand over the past two decades. The Euro will bring even more change. Warehouse districts, industrial parks, a Volvo dealership, and lots of new housing and new McDonald's restaurants speak of Valence's entry into the global economy.

Europe's economic integration of the past quarter-century is evident along the Rhone, long one of Europe's major byways. Nuclear power plants and petrochemical refineries mingle with greenhouses and market gardens, while condos and retirement villas fight for space with the vineyards and orchards on the slopes above.

"I still know people who think in old francs," says Grange, referring to the currency that was replaced in the 1960s. "How will they cope with the Euro?" Nonetheless, she says, the Euro is an important and essential step "necessary for the progress of France."

It's better not to highlight the "inevitable convergence of political and social systems" that will evolve from the Euro, says a French official. "These are extremely emotional, very charged, issues. It is certainly prudent and responsible to focus on the economic consequences, which are substantial and important in and of themselves."

Those consequences may change the dynamics of the entire world. The newly united states of Europe can challenge the United States for primacy in the global economy. Since the Second World War, the U.S. dollar has ruled because it is backed by the world's most powerful economy. The Euro will compete with the dollar on a level playing field. French officials say the new union will enable Europe to better engage the surging economies of Asia, and to present a united front in winning the hundreds of billions of dollars of contracts that will emerge as Asia builds for its future.

But the essential promise of the Euro—that a huge economy with coordinated fiscal and monetary policy will create prosperity—will need to be delivered quickly, if it is to be credible. Already, high unemployment is leading to unrest. France, Italy and Germany have official unemployment rates around 12 per cent. Spain's is 20.5 per cent. This is in stark contrast to Britain, which is staying out of the Euro for now, with its jobless rate of 4.9 per cent.

"We want jobs now!" shouts twenty-four-year-old Didier Bastiani, part of a weeknight crowd of ten thousand or so marching down Paris's Mount Parnassus Boulevard just as the neons come on. Bastiani says the march tonight is a "bit small, but that's OK. You should have been at the Saturday manifestation, the one down by the Bastille. I'm sure we had two hundred thousand people there." Not all the marchers are jobless. Bastiani, a university graduate, has a job that's "not bad." But without the daily demonstrations, he says, "there will be no serious efforts to address the problem." Will the Euro help to create jobs? "Yeah, sure. Logically it should, sometime in the future. But it's a promise, nothing more. We have 15-per-cent unemployment now, today!"

Even so, there is a consensus in France in favour of the Euro, even if it is sometimes grudging rather than enthusiastic. The major parties of the left and the right—Prime Minister Lionel Jospin's Socialists, the centre-right Union for French Democracy, and President Jacques Chirac's Republican Assembly—all back the Euro.

The opposition comes from the far-left Communists, who see the Euro as another example of governments putting the needs of transnational corporations above the needs of the people—and from the far-right National Front, which says the Euro will destroy French identity, lead to a flood of perilous immigration, and leave France at the mercy of foreigners. But for Clarisse Merle, a marketer for a Rhone Valley winery, the Euro "is a necessity against the force of the U.S. dollar." Her firm exports to more than forty countries. "It will make things easier to deal with one currency within Europe."

Olivier Tournaire, another marketer for the winery, has a different view. "I understand it's necessary, but there is also the question of our sovereignty and identity. The ideal would be—have both the Euro and the franc."

Alain Blanc, a lawyer turned business owner in Paris, worries about too close a relationship with Germany. His perception is coloured because German soldiers killed his grandfather and his parents endured "grave hardships" during the Second World War. "But you cannot ignore history. For us, the relationship with Germany has been a defining one. It is desirable and necessary to have Germany as a partner and an ally. But I worry about the complete merger of our destinies, in effect being one country with Germany, even while I accept that the Euro is necessary for our economic future."

What effect will an economically united Europe have on the world? French officials, Canadian diplomats and economists are cautious in their predictions, but believe it will be more positive than negative, particularly in balancing the United States' dominant position in the global economy.

Britain, which along with Sweden and Denmark has decided to stay out of the Euro for now, is the source of some of the strongest criticism against the Euro. A group of leading British business people says the Euro is a fast road to a bureaucratic nightmare in which countries will lose their economic independence for no good reason.

French officials believe the Euro will help shape the global economy into three spheres—the Japanese yen as the currency of choice in Asia; a Euro zone in Western Europe, some parts of Africa, and the parts of Eastern Europe where the Deutschmark now dominates; and a U.S.-dollar zone everywhere else. "That is quite different from the dollar-dominated world of today," says a French official dealing with the Euro. "It will ensure Europe is not a forgotten player, that it has its due place in the world economy."

The harsh road to a borderless world

Edmonton, Alberta, 29 January 1995

T wo Christmases ago, the financial house of Salomon Brothers had a stunning surprise for the employees of its London office. The transnational company was handing out bonuses, generous Christmas bonuses, to one thousand of its workers. Each of those fortunate workers received one million American dollars. Yes, it was unprecedented. But why not? Salomon Brothers had enjoyed a hugely profitable year. It had garnered four billion dollars—four thousand million dollars—in after tax profits.

There was an outcry in Britain from some leftish academics and newspapers like the *Guardian*—the obstinate pockets of resistance who had yet to embrace the wisdom of the Thatcher revolution. There was nary a murmur elsewhere. This, after all, is how the free market was supposed to work. Margaret Thatcher had lowered taxes, privatized large sectors of government, freed business from regulation. Salomon Brothers—a company that produces no tangible goods—had profited handsomely from the movement of money. Each time money changed hands—in an investment, in a sale, in a bond issue, in a little bout of currency speculation—the international financial houses made money. Theirs is a service industry. They like to help their clients make more money, and a company like Salomon Brothers is very good at it. Its profit in Britain in 1993—profit, not revenue—was larger than the national income of some countries.

The four billion dollars it pocketed from its London operations alone exceeded the gross domestic products of Mozambique, Tanzania, Uganda, Bhutan, Guinea-Bissau, Nepal, Burundi, Chad, Madagascar, Sierra Leone, Laos, Malawi, Rwanda, Mali, Burkina Faso, Niger, Haiti, Benin, Central African Republic, Togo, Guinea, Mauritania, Honduras, Lesotho, Zambia, Papua New Guinea, Jordan, Congo, Jamaica, Namibia, Mauritius, and Botswana.

Salomon's profit was greater than the national income of some of the Central Asian republics of the old Soviet Union, and of countries like Albania, but on these we have no accurate data. I cannot think of a better illustration of the New World order that emerged from the collapse of communism.

Its principal feature is the muscular assertion of the power of money. When transnational corporations are larger and more powerful than countries, national borders and the very concept of a nation-state becomes meaningless. The new era of globalization is exactly that: the entire world is just a marketplace, and money flows to where the most profit can be made at the least cost. Thus profitability and economic efficiency become guiding principles. The things governments once used to do—use tax revenues to create a more equitable society, achieve social justice, establish a higher standard of civilization—have little place in this new thinking.

The new order is but another phase in the revolution launched by Margaret Thatcher in Britain and Ronald Reagan in the United States. It sees government as an unnecessary burden, as something that gets in the way of profits and efficiency. The cry carries on today, with demands to get government out of the business of meeting the needs of the citizens it represents.

In this new phase of the Thatcher-Reagan revolution, the loftiest goal of humankind is the pursuit of wealth. The most valued citizens are the most acquisitive, those who are best able to amass wealth with the least interference from the state. This plays well with the extreme connotations of individual freedom that exists in the United States. It is the anarchic freedom, which demands no obligation to society at large. The model of every person for oneself is at the core of unchecked capitalism. If all have the opportunity to make money, why should there be a role for the compassionate state? Thus we are required to question the "affordability" of social programs, yet no one questions the "affordability" of handing out million-dollar bonuses.

The new capitalist orthodoxy is clear: taxes are wrong. Woe betides any government that tries to raise them, to pay for the needs of the poorest and weakest members of society. If Britain had taxed away another billion dollars of Salomon's profit—leaving it with three billion dollars rather than four billion dollars—then the reaction from the halls of capital might have been one of predictable fury. Those billion dollars from one company alone might have gone to provide safer neighbourhoods, better schools, food and shelter for the destitute. Alas, there is little room for such thinking these days. One is dismissed as a "socialist."

Social programs are seen as a drag on the economy, as a hindrance to profitability. It is no longer fashionable to point out social programs are an investment in people, that they are a measure of a society's innate decency. It was Franklin Roosevelt's New Deal that brought social programs to the fore. It was a means of protecting the majority of the population—those unable or unwilling to indulge in the naked pursuit of wealth—from the worst excesses of capitalism.

The aftermath of the Thatcher-Reagan revolution—as expressed by the Republican Party in the United States—is to undo the New Deal, and the mentality of "dependence" it fostered. Rugged individualism meets rugged capitalism, and this is held out as the model for all.

A country like Canada, ranked by the United Nations as the most desirable place to live in the whole world, is an object of ridicule in this fiercely survivalist worldview. If only the federal government would slash social spending, we are told, our country would be all the more prosperous.

We should stop to think about where the excesses of unchecked capitalism will lead. We should think about the sort of society it will foster. What is under attack now is not just the alleged generosity of social programs. It is the basic notion that a civil society ensures a minimal standard of living for its neediest citizens.

If the compassionate state is no longer affordable, what is? A society, in which an economic elite enjoys every advantage, while the majority falls farther behind? The radical-right revolutions—whether led by Thatcher, Reagan, or our own Ralph Klein—have one common factor. They make life much more comfortable for those who are already well off, and much less comfortable for the disadvantaged.

A nineteenth century Prussian philosopher, whose most enduring ideas—progressive income tax, free education for all children—we take for granted today, warned of where these excesses might lead. A world where commercial capital reigns supreme, he wrote, is a world of legalized plunder. That philosopher is today discredited for all the wrong reasons —others made an utter hash of putting his theories into practice— but his words are worth remembering. Why? Because the most ardent advocates of unfettered capitalism would have us revert to the economic structures of a century ago, the exploitative, survival-of-the-fittest economy so ably described by Karl Marx.

In the new era of globalization and international competitiveness, we can in fact find echoes of an older era—the age of colonialism. In the previous century, individual nations enjoyed the fruit of exploiting the territories they colonized. In the new order, transnational investors are the new colonial power. Capital flows in pursuit of least cost and most profit. Countries are played off against one another—give us this break and that advantage, or we will locate elsewhere. Don't raise taxes, or we'll shift our investment out of your country. Do what you like with social programs, but don't raise the cost of doing business.

The most successful colonial powers did not confer wealth on their citizens. The purpose was to sustain an elite. The Indian experience, the one I have most closely studied, illustrates this pattern perfectly. The

British ruling class and the Indian aristocracy joined hands early and often. Each had their privileges protected. There was an enormous transfer of resources and profit out of India to Britain. Yet the ordinary Briton was no better off as a result, nor was the ordinary Indian. One has only to read Charles Dickens to revisit the appalling poverty and social misery of nineteenth century Britain—a country that had grown enormously wealthy from its colonial possessions.

Today's neocolonialism is a little more sophisticated. In the global marketplace, the materials might come from one source, the capital from another, the labour and assembly from yet another. The pressure thus grows in developed countries, to lower costs as much as possible, to lower pay as much as possible, in order to compete with emerging economies. The profits flow to the investing elites and to the owners and managers of the enterprises. Some people will grow immeasurably richer while others will see their standard of living go down.

In our egalitarian country, we may once again see the emergence of a ruling class, with a poorly paid, poorly sheltered service industry to cater to the needs of an economic elite. Go to a nice restaurant in Edmonton, and you might see people with six-figure incomes being served by people who earn six dollars an hour. At one time, this disparity seemed less glaring, because the person earning six dollars an hour still had access to quality health care, quality education, and a sturdy social safety net in times of need. It is these protections that are threatened today by the push for efficiency at all costs, and the "need" to dismantle social spending. The agenda of the radical right may indeed make us more competitive in the global economy, but at what price?

Soccer Night in Kyiv

Kyiv, Ukraine, 12 April 1998

I know I'm in a different country when the Air France jet taxis up to a dilapidated terminal with an enormous fire escape bolted on to the control tower and men with handcarts trundle up to the plane to unload luggage. Welcome to Ukraine, the land of making do. Despite appearances, the luggage is waiting by the time I'm through the border controls. The terminal has the feel of another era, more like a rail station than an airport.

Outside is a blue Moskvitch hatchback: not much compared with the fancy imports that dot the parking lot, but a perfectly good and reliable car that starts and runs no matter what the weather. It'll be a big part of my life for the next week. And I'll exchange a thousand words with Roman, my interpreter, for every word with Vlad, our shy and stoic driver.

Within minutes, we are passing through a landscape that might have been sliced from any part of western Canada where prairie and parkland mingle. From the plane, there was an odd sense of dislocation—the prairie so vast we might have been coming in to land at Regina. But then I saw Kiev, and all thoughts of Regina disappeared. It's a huge city, once the second city of the Soviet Union after Moscow. It has all the grandeur, beauty, and ugliness of its mixed history: the ancient capital of the Rus and a showpiece of Stalinism.

In a few minutes, one can drive from grand buildings in pastel colours and wedding-cake decorations to neighbourhoods with row upon row of apartments—somewhere between a low rise and a high rise, all out of the same mould, almost impossible to tell apart by night. The buildings are a metaphor for life in Kiev. The exterior may be drab and indifferent, but there is a rich interior life. The sullen clerk, the couldn't-care-less paper pusher, may go home to become a warm and loyal parent or friend.

My first glimpse of that interior life comes within hours of arriving in Kiev. Thanks to Edmonton-based historian Bohdan Klid, whose visit to Ukraine coincides with part of mine, Volodya and Tamara Taran have invited us for dinner. He is an artist whose striking rendering of St. Michael recently won a major prize; she is a technician.

Volodya is waiting at the metro station when Bohdan and I arrive. The ride from downtown was smooth and fast. The metro runs far below ground—steeply angled escalators carried us so far we couldn't see the top when we were at the bottom. Then I realized that these were built to shelter people if the missiles of the West ever dropped on Kiev.

We walk a few hundred metres to a housing complex put up only four or five years ago. Yet the entrance is dark and crumbling. These were among the first apartments built to be sold as private property, but the quality of work is very much Soviet-era. Inside the bright and spacious Taran apartment, it's a different story. Volodya's art brings a light of its own to the walls.

Their daughters Yaryna and Mariana are watching cartoons. Yaryna is learning English but is too shy to try with me. Mariana is as curious as any bright five-year-old. Her smile could light up a room. Bohdan and I have brought wine, so the Tarans put the vodka away. I thank them for their generosity in welcoming a stranger. Tamara smiles and waves it away, as though it were the most normal thing in the world. They set a grand table: caviar, cheese, sausage, preserves, and one of the national dishes—potato pancakes, topped with a ragout of chanterelles and other wild mushrooms.

"We picked these mushrooms when we were on holidays in the Carpathian Mountains," says Volodya. "You don't want to pick the local mushrooms," says Tamara. "There weren't many before, but they're everywhere since the Chernobyl accident." The Tarans have ease about them, a genuineness that quickly makes me feel in the company of friends. We talk about their lives, the past, the future, and when I go, Volodya insists on giving me one of his prints. That sense of welcome and warmth can be in complete contrast to a more public or official life.

•   •   •

One night, Roman and I are taking in one of the year's premier sporting events: the quarterfinal of the European Champions Cup of Soccer. The home side, Dinamo Kiev, tied 1–1 in the first of the home-and-home series against one of the world's most powerful teams, Juventus of Turin. There are great hopes riding on the game. If Dinamo win, the country will go nuts, says Roman. So will the Social Democratic Party, which is running an election campaign based on the fact that Dinamo's owner is one of its prime supporters. The party is gambling its campaign on a Dinamo victory.

Security is tight at the perimeter fence, our tickets are checked, and we're through. But that doesn't mean we can see the game. The militia "guarding" the seats has other ideas. The game has started, so they're not letting anyone in. We all have tickets. Our seats are in Sector One, and the tickets have "honoured guest" printed right on them. It doesn't matter. Even though there's strict control at the stadium entrance, even though there's no particular reason to prevent people with tickets from finding their seats, the militia has its own version of busywork. En masse, it is driving back the crowd of elite Ukrainians, closing gates to block access to the seating areas. Imagine getting into Commonwealth Stadium with your ticket, only to be met by police at every stairwell blocking your access to the stands. It is an absurd sight. Women in fur coats, men in expensive leathers, all waving their VIP tickets in the face of the authorities as the militia keeps out the crowd. We can hear the game, but there's no way to see it.

"We can't get in through here; let's try the upper level," says Roman. It's worse. The militia is pushing the gates as far out as they'll go, until people begin to tumble backward down the steps. Spotting a movement at the Sector One gate, Roman and I hurry back down. The militia is trying to push the crowd away, and winning.

Then, one enterprising fellow pushes his son to the top of the gates, and tells the lad to jump down. Confusion in the militia ranks. Seizing the opening, the crowd surges. The militia pushes back. Almost by instinct, the crowd forms into a wedge. We push forward like a rugby pack, feel the militias yield, and we're through! The militia lies dazed on the ground, making no attempt to get back up and stop anyone. They lose, we win. What's the point in fighting? It doesn't seem to matter that their intervention was utterly pointless. One militia officer, with the stupefied look of the vanquished, gets up and starts doing his job—showing people where the Sector One seats begin.

The game is evenly balanced through the first hour, and the eruption of one hundred thousand people when Dinamo ties the game is one of those blood-stirring experiences. A few minutes later, the euphoria is stilled. Juventus turn the game up a notch. Two impossible-to-defend headers off corner kicks, a rocket from an impossible angle and Juventus stride off with 4-1 victory. The place empties fast, all spirit drained from the crowd. The next day Kiev is in mourning. Another dashed hope, in a history of dashed hopes. But the consoling vodka is cheap. The Social Democrats finish fourth.

•　　•　　•

By another of those circuitous connections, Roman and I find ourselves in the home of Yuriy and Tetyana Kostynovy. A friend in Medicine Hat has a brother studying in Ukraine, and Tetyana is one of his professors. I don't want to impose. But Satya Panigrahi, our friend's brother, insists it's no imposition.

He picks us up in his Volvo—Indian students don't do badly in Kiev —and drives us to the Kostynovy flat. Well acquainted now with the Ukrainian fondness for drink—by local practice, a one hundred milligram shot of vodka is a standard beginning, two or three are required for warmth in the damp cold—we stop at a state-run gastronom for two bottles of Finlandia Cranberry vodka.

"Two Satyas!" Tetyana exclaims after the introductions. We are led to a truly amazing table. By now, I have a good idea of what Ukrainian hospitality means. But the Kostynovys' table seems a feast for twenty, not six—different kinds of cold fish, chicken, salads, and an enormous platter of rolled beef stuffed with mushrooms, served on potatoes.

When they learn I'm paying $161 U.S. for a hotel, they turn reproachful. "Why waste money when you have friends? You can stay here!" I explain I'm leaving in two days. Next time, says Tetyana, their home should be my first stop.

The Kostynovys' life has been remarkable. Yuriy was a senior manager at Chernobyl. He earned the highest possible salary in the Soviet Union—2,800 roubles a month—then about $5,000 U.S.

"Everyone knows about Chernobyl the village, but the world does not talk about the city of fifty thousand people that was built at the plant gates." He was one of the first on the scene after the explosion at the Chernobyl nuclear plant. It was all preventable, he says. "The bosses in Moscow wanted too much, too fast. The new generating units were built too close together. We told them we would need a minimum of four months to make sure everything was safe. They wanted it done in a month." Yuriy sustained a massive dose of radiation. It took six years of medical treatment before he could resume a normal life. "The American doctors saved my life."

The first bottle of vodka is gone when we start looking at pictures. There's a picture of whippet-lean Yuriy as a hockey goalie. He played for Dinamo Kiev from 1958 to 1972. "If my career had come later, I might have played against your Canadians." We talk about the legendary 1972 series. And there's absolute agreement on the greatest hockey game of all time—the 3–3 tie between the Soviet Red Army and the Montreal Canadiens in 1975. There are pictures taken with cosmonauts and with other dignitaries visiting Chernobyl. Then we come to a picture of Tetyana on Broadway. "One day in 1993, the American doctors said to me, 'Yura, how would you like to go to America?' I said I'm always ready to go, I thought they were joking. And I said of course, my wife would have to come, and all the family and friends around the table."

The next week, six tickets, passports, and visas arrived. "They showed me off as a medical specimen," says Yura. "All the doctors were amazed I survived." But there was a secret, he says, that the Americans didn't know. "Everyday, when people came off shift at Chernobyl, they had to drink 100 grams of vodka!" he says with a twinkle in his eye. "That's what saved our lives!"

There is only one regret, says Yura. His savings from his job amounted to a six-figure fortune in U.S. dollars at a time when it wasn't possible to buy property. When the Soviet Union imploded the massive and immediate collapse of the rouble rendered his fortune useless.

But regret doesn't mean bitterness. Yura and Tetyana are happy grandparents take pride in the accomplishments of their grown children. The only thing that still gnaws at him is the memory of Chernobyl. "All those lives! All those people! It is so sad, so terribly sad. And none of it needed to happen."

A reasonable facsimile of farce

Kyiv, Ukraine, 29 March 1998

His face growing redder, Roman waves his arms and unleashes a torrent of Ukrainian at the supremely indifferent clerk behind the metal grille. "What kind of image are you giving our country?" he shouts. "Why do you think any foreigners will come here?" His outburst produces the most elaborate shrug I have seen in years. I have to step in and move Roman away before his blood pressure rises any higher. Roman, my interpreter and guide who has become a friend in the few days we have known each other, is incensed more by the clerk's attitude than by the fact Ukraine's leading foreign exchange bank refuses to cash an American Express traveller's cheque. "She doesn't care," he says. "She just doesn't care." Communism may be dead in Ukraine, but its spirit lives on.

With not one but two currency-exchange booths in the lobby of the Hotel Rus, you would think it would be easy to cash a traveller's cheque. It is, if you carry your receipts with you. Otherwise, forget it. Never mind that most travellers leave their receipts at home in case the cheques get lost, carrying only a record of the serial numbers on their travels.

The Ukraine Export-Import Bank demanded original receipts, said the clerk. Until Roman arrived, I had no idea why my cheques weren't cashable. After he got the explanation, and was told a record of the serial numbers wouldn't do, we asked about the alternatives. You could get a cash advance against your Visa card, said the hotel reception. So we go back to the Exim Bank counter and ask. Yes, the clerk admits, it's possible. I offer my Visa card. She puts it into her computer scanner. I can see from the screen that it comes back approved. She returns the card with a shrug even more elaborate than the one that greeted Roman's outburst. "It's no good."

Why? Roman asks.

My signature on the card is faded. Legible but faded. So she can't accept it. Besides, it's a gold card, and she's not sure if she can accept one. Luckily I have an emergency backup: a business credit card I carry for last-resort use if I ever get stuck on a foreign trip, or if something goes wrong with my own card. She examines it for a couple of minutes, looks at the legible signature, sticks it in the machine, tells me I can have a maximum of two hundred U.S. dollars, plus three-per-cent commission, of course. So let me understand, I ask Roman. My traveller's cheques are void because I have no proof I purchased them. My gold card is void because my signature is suspect. But my emergency card is fine, even though I'm suspect in my first two tries. "It's the mentality of the old system," he says.

So I ask the *Journal* to fax my receipts. I ask at the hotel desk in the morning: did a fax arrive for me? No, they say with a welcoming smile. I ask the next morning. Did the fax arrive? "Unfortunately Mr. Das, no," says the lady with another winning smile.

Then I get a call from my friend and colleague Peter Adler, who knows how to work a Soviet-era system—he was one of those Czechs who "got five thousand tanks in exchange for two thousand words" after the 1968 Prague Spring manifesto unleashed a Soviet invasion. Peter has been phoning around in Russian, he says, because the *Journal* was unable over at least several dozen tries to get the fax through. After berating the manager of the Hotel Rus in an elite Russian accent acquired at Moscow State University, Peter learned their fax is broken. He faxed the receipts to the neighbouring Hotel Kievskaya. The Kievskaya sends the fax over to the Rus, which charges me $4.50 even though its own fax is broken. Now can I cash the cheques? No! Only original receipts will do.

So it's off to the embassy. The Canadian Embassy's accountant phones the Export Import Bank, which happens to be Canada's banker. Yes, it's true. New rule. You need an original receipt as proof of purchase. However, I'm welcome to visit their head manager who could offer me tea and have a look at the cheques. Fortunately, a Canadian diplomat has an easier answer: if I sign the cheques over to him, he'll deposit them in his own account and get the money. So that's how Roman, and our driver Vlad, finally got paid for their services.

Roman still wanted to see if we could win over the system. The next morning, he took my fax, a one hundred dollar cheque and my passport to the same hotel money exchange that had refused us. There was a different clerk. "This is an original receipt," he declared pointing at the fax. Without a word, the clerk stamped everything and handed over ninety-eight U.S. dollars. "Won't she get into trouble?" I ask. Roman turns to me, a grin of victory on his face, and shrugs.

Ukraine's eternity of promises unfulfilled

Kyiv, Ukraine, 5 April 1998

On a bitter March day, brisk wind driving gritty snow, Pavlo Trofimovich Polyshchuk pulls down his fur hat and stands behind his sidewalk table with an expectant smile. It is 10 A.M. on a weekday, and customers are few on this frozen street in downtown Kiev. Pavlo, who looks to be in his sixties, will be outdoors the entire day, selling his collection of hand-painted wooden eggs, homemade dolls, and other crafts and curios. It may be cold, but his is a prime spot in the craft market that sets up daily along Andriivsky Uzviz Street. By Canadian standards, Pavlo's existence seems harsh. By today's Ukrainian standards, it's easy street: only three or four dozen people are lucky enough to win such a prize selling spot. Pavlo is a reasonably successful entrepreneur, part of Ukraine's emerging middle class.

"These are all done by my wife," he says, showing a selection of eggs in floral patterns. The eggs are beautiful, and at five hryvnyas ($3.60) each, they seem a bargain. Five hryvnyas is a handsome price in Pavlo's world, and as he makes change for a Canadian visitor, he shows a wallet packed with many more hryvnyas than any pensioner would earn—if pensions were paid on time.

The euphoria of freedom is fading, as Ukrainians wait for the brighter future that is yet to come. In its seventh year of independence, Ukraine is a country waiting to be made—still at the starting gate while its neighbours in Eastern Europe race ahead to reform. "The shock therapy in Poland worked quickly," says Roman Mehedynyuk, twenty-six, a linguistics graduate studying law part-time. "Here, we are still waiting."

Ukraine has the potential to be one of Europe's richest countries, but is doing precious little to achieve its promise. Its rich farmland, mineral wealth, and high levels of education should all make it a success. The fundamentals still aren't in place. Property law, business law, tax law, farm law, all await the attention of legislators. The task of building a country—creating the rule of law, a civil society, a notion of the common good—has yet to be seized by Ukraine's elite. "Everyone is too busy looking after themselves, they have completely abandoned their duty to their fellow citizens," says Yuri Valentinovich Kostynovy, a retired safety supervisor at the Chernobyl nuclear plant. "This is not normal: this is against our character."

Ukraine's formal economy is largely run by the IMF, which advocates massive layoffs in the public sector as the fastest way to create a market economy. Politicians resist, fearing the public backlash.

In all, the Ukraine government owes about $5.2 billion in unpaid wages and pensions to state-sector workers and retirees. Considering a senior teacher or a doctor make about $90 a month—when they're paid—it is easy to imagine how many disrupted lives $5.2 billion represents. Why can't the government pay back wages? Many reasons are offered: shrinking economic production, a contracting economy, corruption, an inability to collect taxes, an unwillingness to pay taxes. One compelling pattern emerges: Ukraine has an economy of complete self-reliance. People do what they must to just get by, awaiting the creation of a more formal and workable economy from the market on the street.

•   •   •

"Here, we haven't gotten rid of the old system yet," says Evgueni Samartsev, a former Communist who runs trade fairs and promotes international education. "People who had power in the old system have power now. We must renovate the whole state system." In the old system, he says, "no one took personal initiative or responsibility for a decision. Every decision kept on passing up the line, to the top." This mentality persists, he says. And some of the key figures in the old system, people accustomed to power or command, have done well for themselves. It shows on the street. A few steps away from Pavlo are the prized possessions of the real beneficiaries of Ukraine's independence: Mercedes, BMW, Ford, and Lexus take their place among the Moskvitch and Ladas of another age. They belong to the new Ukrainians, people who have made a lot of money very quickly even as the old system fell apart.

Answers on how the "new" Ukrainians acquired their wealth are far from clear. There are rumours of stolen aid money, of stolen state property, of a profitable link between politicians and gangsters. But the evidence is anecdotal. The trials that might reveal the truth are unlikely: parliamentarians in Ukraine are immune from prosecution while in office.

Pavlo and the many others like him on Andriivsky Uzviz Street count themselves lucky. They are making decent money, and they are doing better than merely getting by. Those two facts set them apart from many millions of their fellow Ukrainians, for whom the imperatives of coping can bring lives much harder than those of the craft-sellers.

In the evenings in Kiev's metro stations, it's common to see a row of well-dressed people—many of them fresh from other jobs, by the look of them—selling things. Here's a woman in a fur coat with six eggs, two loaves of bread, and two sausages. Here's a man in a suit with several bars of soap, two bottles of shampoo, and some combs. Here's a couple, apparently with connections to the countryside, with potatoes and cabbages all in a heap.

They find customers, but there's little eye contact—as though the buyers and sellers are ashamed they should have to go through this transaction. "They might be teachers, civil servants, even doctors," says a Canadian diplomat. "People do what they have to for survival."

•   •   •

The immense contrast between the Lexus crowd and the government stalls that sell bread by the slice; between pensioners who haven't been paid and restaurants where their entire monthly pension would only buy them a steak dinner, might cause resentment. But that's not enough to fuel social upheaval, says a Canadian diplomat of Ukrainian ancestry. "People here are very accepting."

Canadian historian Bohdan Klid has a stark explanation: "Their spirit was broken, first by the famine, then by Stalinist rule. They've forgotten how to fight back." Younger Ukrainians are starting to ask questions. Petro Kovalenko, an entrepreneur in his twenties, says, "People are too patient here. That's why there's no revolution, no civil strife in Ukraine. If you ask our people to fight for their rights, they turn away. They are here to suffer and complain."

There is much to suffer, and much to complain about. According to official figures, economic output has fallen by 30 per cent in six years. But the numbers only reflect the state industries that have fallen idle; there is no accurate measure of the street-level economic activity, nor of the barter system by which many ordinary people survive. There are more tangible measures. Life expectancy is falling sharply—a combination of social conditions and declining health care. The population is shrinking from a high of fifty-two million as deaths exceed births.

Food is plentiful, but many cannot afford the range of products in the state-run "gastronoms," let alone the private-sector supermarkets. The gastronoms are busier than the supermarkets—they have fewer imported luxury goods—but there are enough people making enough money on the side to keep the supermarkets in business.

• • •

"No one really starves here," says Svetlana Fialova, a veterinarian who sells bull semen to Ukraine farmers. "People have enough food." That food might be something as simple as bread, potatoes, and cabbages or beets, but "meeting the daily caloric requirements is not really a problem," says Dr. Danuta Fedorivna Podkuvska, director of a health region in greater Kiev. Rural people survive on the food they grow on their small private plots—everything from sunflowers for oil to livestock for meat and dairy products. Urban pensioners survive because bread and potatoes are still cheap.

"Everyone has two or three things going on the side," says Roman Zyla, a Canadian scholar studying small business in Ukraine. "No one can really make a go of it on their official salary, even if they do get paid on time."

Pensioners are hard-hit. They receive between thirty-five and sixty dollars a month from the state, about half the salary paid to professionals and about a third less than nurses, office workers, and factory workers receive. Yet chicken costs at least three dollars a kilogram, red meat even more—about six times higher than Soviet-era prices. Staples are more affordable—a decent-quality sausage can be had for one dollar or even less, while a loaf of bread in a state-run supermarket costs about thirty cents. Vodka costs about $1.50 a litre. "Things cost more, but they are now widely available," says Zyla. "And there is an assurance of quality. Today's sausage has real meat, not filler." "The only thing I really want is a little bit more for my pension. The small pension makes it very difficult," says eighty-year-old Sofia, a former nurse who volunteers at the Volodymyr Church.

• • •

Such considerations do not exist for the newly rich Ukrainians. They flaunt their wealth. There are strip clubs, cabarets, casinos, and exclusive bars where the cover charge is a month's wages for a teacher.

Approach a table of the newly wealthy in the expensive Old Fortress restaurant—where main courses run to forty dollars, with vegetables costing extra—and you are likely to be intercepted by bodyguards. When the host of the party of six does agree to an interview, the answers are more coy than illuminating.

"My name? Call me Mel Gibson," he says to uproarious laughter from his companions. He is wealthy "because this is land of opportunity, just like America!"

Despite the uncertainty and the hardship, and nostalgia for Soviet times expressed in a 26-per-cent vote for the Communists in last month's elections, there is a widespread acknowledgement there is no going back to the past.

In Soviet times, Volodya Taran was a state-supported artist. He still works on his art, but he had to get a job to pay the bills. For Volodya and his wife Tamara, life is different today: the old certainties of a cradle-to-grave socialist system are gone, but so are the restrictions, the repression, and the overwhelming hand of authority. "Some things are better; some things are not," says Tamara. But none of them wants to go back to the old days. Volodya can sell paintings, and they bought their apartment upon the advent of privatization, before massive inflation set in, so they consider themselves better off than many. Their fourteen-year-old daughter Yaryna goes to a good state-run school. Whatever the difficulties the underpaid teachers might face and however budgets have been cut, she is flourishing in an academic program in which she learns, among other subjects, five languages: Ukrainian, Russian, English, French, and German. Yaryna has little memory of Soviet times, and their five-year-old Mariana was born after independence. "Our daughters will have a better future," says Tamara.

That future might be a long time coming. Everyone speaks of a "transition period," but young Ukrainians especially question why the transition is taking so long. "My brother went to Poland to find a job, things are much better there," says Serhi, twenty-two, a student whose family hails from western Ukraine. The quality of education in Ukraine is high, says Samartsev. The difficulty is no one has been taught to think critically, to challenge authority. Samartsev, thirty-seven, now runs a nongovernmental organization that arranges foreign education for Ukraine's top students, more to give them an idea of how free countries work. He was once a true believer: a Communist Party student leader at Kiev University and later a leader of Komsomol, the Communist youth organization. "The generation of young people now, the ones who are younger than me, really need to be trained abroad to change their way of thinking," says Samartsev. The Gorbachev era was a change in direction because "the movement to more democracy and more openness was well-received by all of society." But that change had no real context, no indication of what sort of future it would lead to. The same can be said of Ukraine today. "Even this is better than the past. The old ideology is destroyed, there can never be a return to the Soviet era."

Ukraine's recent election reflects that search for a new beginning. Of the 225 directly elected seats—another 225 are awarded by proportional representation—Communists won the largest single bloc. Candidates not affiliated with any of the thirty parties contesting the vote won more than half the seats—at least 114. Whoever tries to form a government will have to negotiate with these independents, whose election reflects disenchantment with formal parties and the often-shady characters that run them.

Liudmyla Serhiivna Levchenko, who has an unfinished doctorate at Carleton University, runs a project that's vital to building Ukraine's future, one that is trying to lay the foundations for civil society and a democracy that combines the market economy and social safety net found in most western countries. She directs the Canada Ukraine Legislative Co-operation Project, which is drafting democratic laws for Ukraine one sector at a time—and lobbying Parliament to get them passed.

This Canadian-funded framework, once complete, will offer laws covering agriculture, land reform, private property, energy, management, taxation, and general lawmaking. Canadian diplomats say it "may be the most important initiative" of all the foreign-assistance projects in Ukraine.

Levchenko has no illusions about the complexity of the project, which was developed with the University of Alberta's Canadian Institute of Ukrainian Studies. She says the Czech Republic, Poland, and other countries in the region are more successful than Ukraine because they had their independence until the Second World War.

Because there was no free flow of information from other countries, Levchenko and others of her generation—she graduated from Kiev University in 1984—were brought up to believe that the state would care for all their needs from birth to death. "We really used to believe in the system," says Levchenko. "We used to believe that the political leadership would do their best." Now, it's hard to imagine what the best alternatives are, even to instill basic capitalist concepts like private property and individual ownership. "Everybody is a product of that old system, but nobody wants to live in that any more," says Levchenko. "But we do not really know the best way to move forward, or what the best alternatives are."

The Memory of Blood at Babi Yar

Babi Yar, Ukraine, 22 March 1998

E ven on a grey day, wind-driven snow bending the budding branches, it seems like another of Kyiv's many pleasant parks: lots of trees, an imposing official building at one side, a factory of some sort at another, an open space enclosed by busy streets. There's a pleasant U-shaped ravine, a fairly shallow one, just enough for kids on a toboggan to start working up speed before reaching flat ground—a toddler's slope. Then you notice the ravine is completely enclosed by a hedge. And the vast monument rising above, formless from a distance, begins to convey a terrible meaning. What appeared from afar to be a black monolith becomes a cascade of human terror: the sculptors convey a sense of the ominous; their art tries to speak the unspeakable. And finally, you arrive at the base of the monument, and the inscriptions in Cyrillic and Hebrew: Babi Yar.

What happened here is an act that even today is too monstrous to comprehend.

I walked through a gap in the hedge, look over the ravine and begin to weep. My tears fall to the snowy slope, to mingle in the ground with the memory of blood. In this spot, in this ravine, the soldiers of Nazi Germany murdered one hundred thousand Ukrainians, nearly all of them Jews.

Babi Yar may have been the single worst atrocity outside the death camps in the Holocaust that consumed most of European Jewry, the Holocaust that killed eleven million people in central and Eastern Europe. It looks so innocent now, a place of such peace. You can imagine how leafy it would be in summer. Such are the places where evil is done. An ordinary ravine in a grand city becomes a monument to a horror that can never be undone.

Kyiv resisted for more than two months before the Nazis conquered it in September 1941. Then came the horror of Babi Yar. The mind tries to understand how one group of human beings, standing armed on the lip of the ravine, could shoot other humans driven to the low ground below: how a group of soldiers could in any way think they were fighting a war when they were ordered to slaughter the terror-stricken civilians below. There could be no challenge to Nazi "superiority." Dinamo Kiev won a soccer game against the conquerors. The next day the victorious Ukrainians were slaughtered at Babi Yar.

Horrific though Babi Yar was, it was just another chapter in the catalogue of calamity that has befallen Ukraine throughout this century. The Stalinist famine that starved millions, the various purges and terrors, the rule of brutality that forced Ukrainians to live the hardest of lives, the wars forced on them by others: the scope of suffering in this country is appalling.

Outside a school I visited this week is a stone marker with the pictures of four boys: former students killed in the Afghanistan war. You see the toll of the century on the faces of older people. They reflect lives lived intensely in the most harrowing of circumstances.

But there is something more. There is also a sense of hope. The country has only been independent for six years, and the people I have talked to know well there will be many difficulties and trials ahead. There is a unanimous feeling that Ukrainians are at last their own masters, they will no longer be the victims of a fate beyond their hands.

From the darkness of Babi Yar I moved into the light of the Sunday service at the Volodymyr church, savouring the emotions of a language I could not understand as the stirring rhythms of the Orthodox liturgy rose towards the dominant portrait of the Mother of God. The faces were a wonder to see. Weathered, hardened faces yielding to a communal sense of peace, the stirrings of a quiet joy. In purple and gold robes, the white-bearded Patriarch of the Ukraine led the service, flanked by two equally resplendent high priests and rows of others in dazzling formal vestments. Incense wafted from the censers as people moved around the church to light candles, kiss portraits of the divine mother and of Jesus, say special prayers at the relics of saints.

I met eighty-year-old Sofia, who was serving water to those who had just left the communion. Her husband was a Soviet soldier killed in the Second World War. She has been coming to this church ever since, often in secret, now openly. "I am not well; my life is very hard," she said. "But I know all will be well, because now we are allowed to believe in God." She comes to serve the Virgin Mary whom she started seeing in visions fifty years ago. She has waited a long time for Ukraine to awaken to freedom. And even though her meagre pension makes life a struggle, "we can have faith. "Without faith it is very, very hard to live."

You too can live in the Victorian Age

Singapore, 14 August 1995

Singapore's remarkable campaign against media "irresponsibility" recorded yet another victory this month when a civil court in the city-state awarded damages of more than one million dollars Cdn against the newspaper *International Herald Tribune.* Edited in Paris and printed in more than a dozen cities, the *Herald-Tribune* is the one truly global newspaper. You can pick it up just about everywhere. It's what the British would call a serious newspaper, aimed at a cosmopolitan English-speaking elite.

But in Singapore, it joins a list of miscreants that includes the Asian edition of the Wall Street Journal, Asia's premier newsmagazine *Far Eastern Economic Review,* and the international news and business magazine the *Economist.*

All these journals have offended Senior Minister Lee Kuan Yew and/or his family and associates, by obliquely suggesting, for instance, that courts are used to intimidate the media in Singapore, or implying Lee's son rose to lead the country on any basis other than sheer merit. It particularly offends when anyone suggests Singapore is dictatorial, authoritarian, or anything other than a just and efficient democracy— one where responsibilities and rights go hand in hand.

Lee presents this as the difference between Asian values—promoting the common good—and decadent Western individualism. This fundamental division is at the heart of the disagreement about human rights between many Western countries and Asian countries like Singapore and Malaysia. In fact, it's subtler. It's a clash between two distinct sets of western values: the one that evolved from the British Empire, and the more individual culture of North America.

Singapore, like other societies affected by British rule, is in essence a society of Victorian values and aspirations. I know. If my family hadn't moved to Canada, I might have become an Asian Victorian.

When Captain Fernandes came striding down the aisle, barking questions with a no-nonsense glare, it paid to have a ready answer. If you did, he gave an approving nod and passed on to the next boy. If you didn't, it was one swift stroke with the metal edge of the ruler on your outstretched hand.

My old teacher in a long-ago childhood in eastern India was entrusted with the moral and physical education of boys in their formative years. Rights and privileges were to be earned. Responsibility and discipline came first. There are only three principles one needs to know to lead a proper life, he told us: "trust begets trust; do unto others as you would have them do unto you; there are some rules."

It was up to you to figure out what those rules were, but a chap who followed the first two principles could readily understand the third. My early education was a product of Empire. India was independent, the British were long gone, but the "best" schools turned out boys (and seldom girls) who would one day grow up to rule the Waves. (It's remarkable just how pervasive an education it was. My friend Michael Cooke went to a school in Lancashire founded by John of Gaunt, literally half a world away from my school in India, yet we have a good many experiences in common.)

Such elite formation comes with a sense of noblesse oblige. The ruling elite knows better than the "riffraff," as a Singapore journalist once told me, what is really good for the masses. Genuine, workable democracy is for well-informed, educated, responsible, and upstanding people—otherwise, you have mob rule. What on earth could be wrong, she asked, with a capable and well-informed elite acting for the common good? And who better than the brightest and the best to shape and define that good?

In this view, Singapore's elite is almost entirely in step with the Victorian ruling class. They cannot see that anyone would abandon a prosperous, clean, orderly, and disciplined society, one in which people behave decorously, in favour of the licentious society of individualism that they consider as the defining characteristic of North America and Britain. In this view, accusations of dictatorship rankle the most because Singapore's government upholds—some would say to excess—the rule of law. Suing offending newspapers is a more civilized and elegant variation of the Victorian penchant for horsewhipping scurrilous editors. Far from considering itself out of step, the ruling elite of Singapore proudly advances the banner of neo-Victorianism and waits for the Britons and North Americans to come back to their senses.

Why the world took the road to Melaka

Melaka, Malaysia, 10 February 1996

I am on a sunbaked hilltop in Melaka, standing below a handless statue of St. Francis Xavier, a hilltop that has absorbed the blood of many invaders and conquerors: Portuguese, Dutch, English. Beyond the ruined church, beyond the replica of the ship that brought the admiral Alfonso d'Albuquerque here in 1511 to win Malaysia to Portuguese rule, lies the Straits of Malacca. It is perhaps the richest and busiest sea-lane in human history. It carried the spice trade, the silk trade, and all the riches that flowed to fuel the world's commerce in bygone centuries.

On this day, it looks busy as a freeway. Through the haze of thirty-two-degree midday heat, the horizon reveals a line of oil tankers passing through, their massive forms followed by the smaller shapes of roll-on roll-off container ships, driving the engine of trade that is once again making Asia the heart of the world's economy, and Malaysia one of the richest countries in Asia.

That prosperity is readily visible as the eye travels to Melaka's waterfront, once a rendezvous for all the principal languages and cultures of the world, a gateway port to the riches that lay in the dense forests beyond. It is difficult to say what that waterfront might have looked like in a bygone age—a sprawling air-conditioned mall with a cineplex, and high-rise condos still in their construction cladding covers it. The attraction of Melaka started with its strategic location, but in British times, new sources of trade and wealth opened up. Rubber trees arrived from Brazil; oil palms from West Africa, tin came from the ground of Malaysia itself.

Seekers of nostalgia may look back with fondness to a colonial past, where the good life of the ruler was unrivalled in its indolence and ease. There is little such nostalgia in the hearts of many Malaysians, for whom the past was anything but sweet. Like Albertans of the 1970s, they are filled with heady power of a surging economy, the unsinkable optimism that tomorrow will always be better than today, their very best years are still to come.

There is an old Malaysia to be found, if not in an oppressive lifestyle, in a legacy of architecture and urban geography that vividly captures the evolution of life in this once-great port that has become a pleasant provincial town.

The European presence—all of it—is seen in the seventeenth- century Dutch state house, in the ruins of the Portuguese fortress A Famosa and in the polished stone fountain of the Victoria memorial—erected by grateful traders to mark yet another outpost of the empire on which the sun never set. A couple of blocks away lie the markers of the parallel civilization, the world the colonisers conquered. The life of that age is to be seen in the seventeenth century Chen Hoon Teng temple, the oldest Chinese temple on the Malay Peninsula, and in the streets around. Here are the original homes of the *peranakan*, the Malaysian-born Chinese who are descended from the earliest traders and settlers. Even the Kling Mosque, established by Muslim traders from India, has a Chinese-style pagoda as its minaret.

The past has a tangible presence in these streets, in its mood, its styles; utterly separate from the sterility of mall culture. These are streets that bespeak the history of the country, for Melaka is where Malaysia began. There were trading cities before it, to be sure, way stations and markets in the peninsulas and archipelagos that filled in the spaces east of India and south of China.

If there is such a thing as a founding moment, a time and place in history where the seeds of a country were planted, it was in Melaka in 1403. Like all good stories, this one begins with a prince. He arrived in Melaka a fugitive, fleeing the unsuccessful rebellion he launched against his uncle, the Maharaja of Palembang. He was of the Hindu royal house that ruled the huge island of Sumatra, and he was modestly named Parameswara (The Supreme Divinity).

He came ashore off the straits of Malacca, took rest in a cane grove, and asked a local what the trees were called: melaka, came the reply. Later on, those canes would contribute to the riches of European empires. When the British ruled Melaka, they ran it from Calcutta, and set up factories in India to process the cane. Malacca walking sticks were known the world over, and Malacca rattan produced the most sought-after furniture.

Parameswara, though, had other things on his mind—his vengeful uncle, for instance. He needed allies; he needed a base. Both came in the form of the Chinese admiral Cheng Ho, who arrived in 1405 as an emissary of the Ming emperor: carrying, among other things, the Islamic faith. Parameswara converted to Islam, and looking for an appropriate earthly name. He chose to style himself after Alexander the Great, turning the Greek Mega Aleksandros to the Islamic Megad Iskandar Shah.

Within a generation, this alliance between a Hindu Sumatran prince turned Muslim and the Ming emperor of China turned into a flourishing relationship. Together, they made Melaka one of Asia's principal trade centres. The pact was sealed a generation later, when Iskandar Shah's successor Ahmad Shah married the Chinese Princess Li Ping Ho—a match that also sealed Malaysia's destiny as a multicultural country, one of the world's natural meeting points and melting pots.

It is that blend of influences and elements that makes Malaysia so familiar and attractive to a Canadian, and Melaka is an easy and approachable way to gain admission to a stimulating culture and country. It is in some ways a mirror to our country, a search for a shared communal life from many sources.

How the new economy gives women a life

Kuala Lumpur, Malaysia, 15 January 1996

When Dr. Mahani Zainal Abidin talks about her country, she speaks with all the crispness and authority of a scholar who obtained her PhD at the University of London. The only unexpected factor is she is a woman in a Muslim majority country where Islam is the state religion—but Malaysia is not a country that is given to stereotypes. Far from being an exception, Mahani is typical of many Malaysian women who have made a professional career. Democracy and economic growth have given women more freedom than they would have enjoyed in a traditional Muslim society.

Because of Malaysia's commitment to becoming a fully developed country by 2020, there is little room for attitudes that would keep women at home to serve the whims of men. Malaysia has depended on women for its development, unlike Saudi Arabia or the Gulf States whose rules would rather import foreign workers than give women economic and educational independence. About 60 per cent of factory workers are women—they dominate the electronics industry, while male workers are concentrated in the automotive sector, for instance. Nearly half of all Malaysian women are in the labour force.

And while the image of Islamic countries is one of subservient women with no rights, there is nothing in the religion itself to justify typically oppressive male behaviour, says Rashidah Abdullah, a member of the rights advocacy group Sisters in Islam. Social and cultural traditions become confused with religious teaching to justify male domination. "Islam is not an obstacle to economic development," says Rashidah.

In fact, there is a clear separation between government policies and any restrictions that might be imposed for social or cultural reasons. Since 1975, Malaysia has practised pay equity in the public sector and most of the private sector has caught up. Income disparities still exist in unskilled labour, and the private sector often restricts women in "opportunities for advancement and promotion."

Open education has been an enormous advantage in giving women the opportunity to take control of their own lives. School enrolment up to Grade eleven (the end of secondary school) is roughly equal between boys and girls. When it comes to university, though, there's a quota system in place to ensure each gender is proportionately represented. If it weren't for gender quotas, "girls would get the vast majority of the spots," says Rashidah, "because girls perform better academically than boys."

Women are slow to advance in the best-paying professions, but the gap is narrowing. In 1994, a quarter of all doctors were women, as were a third of all lawyers and university teachers. Mahani, a professor at the University of Malaysia's faculty of economics and administration, says legal and illegal immigration has been a help to many Malay women. For semiskilled workers, it means better jobs because the immigrants occupy positions in the lowest fifth of the economy. For middle-class Malay women, she says, the proliferation of Indonesian immigrants makes it easy to hire nannies and housemaids.

While it's easy to point to women's equality and progress in a big city like the national capital Kuala Lumpur, it's much harder to break traditional attitudes in rural areas. An Islamic party that rules the northern state of Kelantan, for instance, is trying to introduce restrictions on women and using religion—wrongly, in Rashidah's view—to justify it. "The man is still the undisputed leader of the family. The woman's role is to provide a harmonious home life, even when she works full-time outside the home," says Rashidah, who is also director of the Asian-Pacific Resource and Research Centre for Women.

The contrast in urban areas is clear. One day in December, the *New Straits Times* reported the case of a suburban Kuala Lumpur man who sexually assaulted his teenage daughter. The man's defence was that this was a fantasy concocted by her. He was sentenced to ten years imprisonment and a dozen strokes of the cane. In other Muslim majority countries, courts place much more weight on a man's evidence. In Malaysia, the criminal justice system is strictly secular, operating on the procedures and rules of evidence common to most Commonwealth democracies.

Reproductive choice is restricted as well. "Especially in rural areas," Rashidah says, "the husband will not permit his wife to take modern forms of contraception." There is also a tendency to turn a blind eye to physical abuse even though the government has strict laws to protect women. "Women may live longer, but they suffer more."

But even in rural areas, the surging economy brings change in unexpected ways, often in exposure to modern ideas and ways of life. Malaysian Airlines is one example. In the past, says a flight director with twenty-one years of on-board experience, there were fewer routes, and flight attendants came from fairly affluent urban backgrounds. In the new economy, people come from all sorts of backgrounds. "We hire women who have grown up in the *kampung* (village) and we train them to deal with people from all sorts of cultures, speaking many different languages."

For most, work at the airline is their first exposure to international travel. Someone who might have never lived in a large city before ends up working a long-haul flight that goes from Malaysia to South Africa and Argentina. After this cosmopolitan experience, women literally bring a new world home to the village they might have spent their whole lives in at the time of their grandmothers' generation.

The Japan Hiro yearned to find

Ubud, Indonesia, 16 August 1998

His fingers curled around a cup of tea, Hiro gazed across the vivid green of central Bali: terraced ricefields, the rise and fall of hills, the morning air fragrant with *champaka* and *kambhoja* blossoms from the surrounding garden.

Mornings were often like this in the three weeks Hiro and I were neighbours in early 1992. We would come down from the cottages to the breakfast veranda at our rustic hotel, passing the fishpond, tossing a piece of fruit to the pet monkey. Hiro had the sort of placidity that comes from an undiluted sense of peace. There is, he would say, perfection here: smoky clouds across a range of faraway hills, a sudden flight of white birds across an intensely blue sky. "I do not want to go back."

"Back" meant going back to Japan. To the expectations parents have of an eldest son. To a life of pressure and success and achievement. He knew he would have to, of course, once the money ran out. But he tried to put off that day as long as he could.

He had come to Indonesia to find what he could not in Japan—an inner calm that arises from being at peace with yourself. Here, far from the realities of his world, he finally understood what Japanese poets and writers talked about. "Now I know what Basho felt," he said as the gathering sun gilded the moisture on the breeze-stirred stalks of ripening rice. He was a relatively young man, somewhere between university and a committed start to a career. With their parents' permission, if not wholehearted blessing, Hiro and his wife were on an extended break from the expected transition—pressure-packed education to pressure-packed job. He knew he would have to go back, but he wondered if the Japan he had left was really worth going back to.

The pursuit of success didn't leave room for pursuits that enriched the mind and soul. "Maybe my country will change," he said with a quiet laugh—half-mocking, half-sad. But he feared it wouldn't—unless other Japanese could perceive, as he had come to, that the race to material affluence could never be an end in itself. I thought of Hiro this week as the Japanese economy sank into full recession—its first real setback in the amazing run of ever-expanding wealth during the last four decades.

Will this be the shock Hiro dreamed of—the one that would lead Japan on a necessary contemplation of its soul? As much as political or economic restructuring, thoughtful Japanese have for some years believed their country needs its soul reshaped. The feeling that there must be something more to life is not new or unique. It lies just below the surface of Japan's frenetic modernity—a longing for the simpler, calmer, life-affirming streams of Japanese culture.

To Hiro, modern Japan's pursuit of prosperity appeared to go against his nature. And yet there were dangers in looking to the past. Like other modern Japanese, Hiro learned militarism was a national disease—like an alcoholic who must forswear strong drink forever, Japan should never again look to a past that glorified military conquest and violence against other nations.

In their flight from that past, had other, more benevolent aspects been abandoned? Hiro feared they had. Only two human lifetimes ago, Japan was a closed society. Impenetrable to the outside world, it was the sort of feudal society that disappeared in Europe centuries ago, run by a warlike aristocratic elite. And within the lifetimes of many Japanese still living, the divine right of kings was unchallenged—the emperor was a god. Japan fled that past because of the singular horror of the Second World War, but Hiro thought one day Japanese people would have to revisit their past—to embrace what was good, to rediscover the currents that shaped and nurtured a country's soul.

Perhaps the economic shock will bring that change—not just to Japan, but to the countries so intertwined with its destiny. That includes us. We are more tied to Japan than many may imagine—everything from borrowed money to courted investments to coveted market for our goods.

A severe economic crisis in Japan will inevitably bring one to Canada—such is the nature of the free-trading global economy. Our society, too, could use some of the introspection and reflection Hiro longed to see in Japan. Here as well, a sense of community sometimes seems overwhelmed by the untempered pursuit of materialism and acquisition. A sense of perspective, a sense of balance, often eludes us. Perhaps an economic shock is one way of finding equilibrium, of rediscovering what matters most. Is serenity anything more than knowing and accepting who you are?

Japan hears the sound of one hand clapping

Tokyo, Japan, 15 November 1997

"Please take the next train from here and go two stops," says Mr. Komatsu, who has come two platforms and at least a couple of hundred metres out of his way to help a Canadian traveller navigate the Tokyo subway. "That will take you directly to the stop in front of the Foreign Ministry. The train will arrive here at 9:46."

And with a couple of bows, he is off at a trot to catch his own train. The train rushes in exactly as 9:45 turns to 9:46 on the platform's digital clock. Thirty seconds to load, and it's off again. Like everything else in Tokyo, the mass transit system is a model of cleanliness and efficiency: the envy of Asia and a reflection of one of the highest standards of civilization in the world.

Devastated by an earthquake in 1923, burned to the ground in the firestorm set off by American bombers during the Second World War, modern Tokyo has the look and the feel of a global capital. It has absolutely everything, and there is no such concept as second best.

The pastries and bread in many French bakeries would be the envy of many Parisian boulangers. The acres of marble in the department stores, the aisles full of the latest designer fashions and perfumes, the giant television screens on the sides of buildings, the busy and animated street life in every neighbourhood—all reflect the success of a massively prosperous society.

And it is all the more remarkable to think this prosperity arose from virtually nothing: at the end of the Second World War, Japan was utterly defeated, the land in ruin, morally and psychologically devastated.

Despite every trapping of wealth and success, Japan is consumed by a feeling of: what next? It is the feeling the postwar evolution of Japan has run its course, that more of the same is neither desirable nor tenable.

The remaking of Japan after the war was the second great reshaping of the country in a short span of history. The end of military dictatorship and the return of the imperial family to power in the Meiji Restoration of 1868 opened Japan to the world after more than 250 years of insular isolation. Japan took the world by storm, transforming itself from a feudal, agrarian, militaristic society to a feudal, industrial, and militaristic one.

The war, the American occupation, and Douglas MacArthur's regency brought yet another transformation: into a pacifist, democratic society that became the industrial powerhouse of the world. Using its most important resource—its people—Japan created what is known worldwide as the Japanese economic miracle.

Japan's economy accounts for nearly a fifth of global economic activity. It is the largest potential investor in the world, with $310 billion in foreign exchange reserves. Japanese lending is a huge part of the world economic engine: through the 1980s and 1990s, it financed much of the one billion dollars the United States borrowed daily to cover its deficit and debt.

Japan is the world's third-largest trading nation and has five of the world's top ten commercial banks. The dominance of Japan's transnational corporations is reflected in one telling statistic: in 1996, Canada's total merchandise exports reached $275 billion. Mitsubishi Corporation's annual sales that year were $260 billion. And Japan leads the world in development assistance, giving out twenty billion dollars in 1995. All this is reflected in a national income of $45,000 per capita.

Converted to a purchasing power parity model—a reflection of the quantity of goods and services a currency can buy—Japan's per capita national income is $31,500, about $2,800 per head higher than Canada's.

Yet among Japan's leaders, among the thinkers, reflected daily in Japanese media, there is the feeling the country needs a third revolution: a change in direction on the scale of the Meiji Restoration and the MacArthur Regency. Perhaps it is the approach of the millennium, or the fact that Japan as a fully developed country has reached a plateau.

The feeling is enhanced by an ageing population, higher health costs, increasing budget deficits. It's something people feel in their bones, says Canadian banker Kenneth Courtis, a vice-president and global economic strategist with Deutsche Bank. "Suddenly, the Japanese think they're two feet tall and the Americans are ten feet tall. They think they can't do anything right."

Part of that shock comes from the last global recession, in which Japanese unemployment peaked at 3 1/2 per cent last summer—a cataclysm in a full-employment economy in which every able-bodied person who wanted to work could be sure of having a job. Suddenly, the Japanese model of a secure, high-wage, high-productivity economy was called into question. More importantly, Japanese people began to wonder if their society was worth being proud of.

"We know we have to make changes," says Koichiro Ejiri, senior advisor to the board of Mitsui and Company and former chair and chief executive of the transnational corporation. The difficulty is in finding the political will to do so. Japan's consensus system of decision-making, the ˆ, is quite literally a circular affair. A circle of managers contributes to the final decision, and everyone's input is accommodated.

While legislators and business leaders—who often work hand-in-glove—agree economic and political reforms might be necessary to redirect Japan, "we have a lack of strong leadership," says a director of Nippon Steel Corporation.

An executive with Matsushita Electric Industrial envies the relative ease with which the Government of Alberta can push through its model of economic restructuring. "This would be very difficult to achieve in Japan."

Writing in the magazine *Look Japan*, Mitsubishi Corporation's Managing Director Akita Osamu sets out the challenge: "The greatest impact of [economic liberalization, a borderless economy] will be to force Japanese corporations to undergo dramatic reforms in their way of management."

John Tennant, Canada's acting ambassador in Tokyo, says many countries would love to have Japan's problems. It may not be as easy to sustain the Japanese economic miracle, but it's still one of the most prosperous countries in the world.

Courtis agrees Japan's abiding anxiety is deeper than it needs to be. The worries—brought on by the recession, the tensions of constant trade sniping with the United States—are really a blip in a big-picture view. "For nearly all of its history, Japan has been shaped by its relationship with China."

Now China "is on the move again, and Japan knows it has to change," just to prevent itself from being overwhelmed by China. Courtis believes Japan's greatest asset has been its people: despite the pressures of an ageing population, he is confident Japan will find a way forward.

In the past, part of the solution has been Japan's ability to invest in other countries and live off the proceeds—in effect, exporting jobs. About 28 per cent of Japan's industrial production is now overseas, a "hollowing out" of the domestic economy has enabled the highest wage jobs to stay in Japan. It may be necessary to bring some of those jobs back to Japan to restore full employment—or Japan could invest even more, and create more substantial profits to finance its domestic needs.

Mel MacDonald, minister-counsellor at the Canadian Embassy in Tokyo, says some of the changes may come from the millions of Japanese now travelling abroad. "They see life in Canada, they see the prices in other countries, they see how the world operates; that creates some of the momentum for change. You never had discount stores in Japan before. Now, it's an extremely competitive market."

Yet a market-driven change, important though it may be, is not nearly enough. In its essence, Japan is a nation in search of its soul. It will surely find a new economic direction—everything about Japan's history points to an astonishing capacity for resilience; its cultural homogeneity gives it a singular ability to enforce collective decision-making, once the decisions are actually made. That very homogeneity is also a barrier—a border of identity that prevents strident individualism from asserting itself. The new Japan is really seeking a balance between the individual and the collective, between public and private personas—to redefine its concepts of borders within an increasingly borderless world.

Why China might choke on
Hong Kong's democracy

Hong Kong Special Administrative Region, China, 7 June 1998

I n a quiet but steely voice, Martin Lee insisted Britain honour the
guarantees of democracy it promised Hong Kong—anything less
would be a breach of trust. It was the winter of 1992. And as the leader
of Hong Kong's most prominent democracy movement talked to me in
the Canadian commission's offices, it was hard to find a freer place on
earth. Hong Kong never had democracy, but it was spectacularly free.
Looking out the window at the busy, sunlit harbour, the jumble of
Kowloon across the water, it appeared impossible this place would one
day succumb to totalitarian rulers.

And thanks to people like Lee, it hasn't. In the end, the British
promises weren't kept. The last governor, Chris Patten, fought valiantly
for the spirit if not the letter of the Sino-British accord, only to be sold
out by the pragmatists within the British government and bureaucracy
—people who regarded Patten's old-fashioned sense of honour, duty, and
calling to be rather pointless if not utterly embarrassing. That's why it
was so satisfying to see the pictures of Martin Lee popping champagne
a few days ago, celebrating the democrats' sweep of the handful of
contested seats available in the legislature. China has engineered the rules
so its appointees will have the majority, but there is no doubt as to

whom has real legitimacy, and who won with the votes of ordinary citizens.

As the first anniversary of Hong Kong's return to Chinese rule approaches, its democracy is alive and well. In fact, it's easy to wonder whether Hong Kong is turning out to be a poison pill for China's autocrats. By absorbing Hong Kong, they have allowed the flame of freedom to burn brighter within China itself.

Last year, when the traditional candlelit gathering in Hong Kong commemorated the June 1989 massacre of democrats in Beijing's Tiananmen Square, organizers wondered whether it would be the last. It wasn't. On Thursday night, forty thousand people gathered in Hong Kong to remember the killings—and all that the Chinese authorities could do was to forbid a permanent memorial.

And for the first time within China proper, the voice of the dissidents Beijing worked so long to silence was in full throat. Wei Jingsheng, jailed fifteen years for putting up posters on Beijing's Democracy Wall, sent a recorded message. Wang Dan, one of the leaders who survived the Tiananmen massacre, spoke on a phone line from the United States.

In a direct challenge to Beijing, he declared "Hong Kong will be the bedrock of the democratic movement in China." And Wei told the crowd what Beijing's autocrats must shudder to hear: "If Hong Kong people continue fighting for the democratic movement in China, the whole of China will ultimately benefit." It was the first time a Tiananmen anniversary had been marked on Chinese soil.

Hong Kong's democracy surge puts China in a dilemma. Any overt crackdown would sap business confidence—billions of dollars would quickly find feet.

As it is, Hong Kong's economy is sagging, due largely to Beijing's stubborn decision to artificially peg the value of the Hong Kong dollar to the U.S. dollar, rather than letting the Hong Kong currency find its own value in the global market. As a result, the Hong Kong dollar is no longer competitive against the devalued Japanese yen, and hugely expensive against any battered Southeast Asian currency.

Hong Kong has effectively priced itself out of the market—the Asian tourism that has sustained much of the street-level economy is gone, and it's unlikely to come back until Hong Kong is affordable once more.

But if China doesn't crack down, then what? Beijing is confronted with the uncomfortable spectacle of Hong Kong's defiant democracy. In the year since Hong Kong reverted to Chinese rule, democratic forces have become stronger rather than weaker. Beijing gambled Hong Kong people wouldn't care about democracy, they would get on with the business of making money. Yet every one of its ham-handed pressure tactics —stacking the decks with appointees so elected democrats can't hold a majority in the legislature, efforts to tame a traditionally free and boisterous press—have met considerable resistance.

And to top it all off, the Asian crisis offers ample proof the future does not belong to a corrupt and cynical system of government that enriches the elite while throwing a handful of development and comforts to the poor. The downfall of Suharto's Indonesia is all the proof that's needed. The old Asian equation—that capitalism can flourish within a dictatorial system—was shattered by Indonesia.

And as Hong Kong's democracy gains vigour, the allegedly communist Chinese government in Beijing must wonder if its own brand of authoritarian crony capitalism is about to meet the dustbin of history.

What the other China's money can't buy

Taipei, Republic of China, 7 December 1997

Nestled in the hills surrounding Taipei, the Grand Hotel is every inch a relic of a bygone age. Its acres of red carpets, its gaudy decorations, its high-ceilinged public rooms, have the look of a fading Hollywood set of a millionaires' private club.

That impression is not far from the reality. Once upon a time, this was the haven for a very privileged elite, the friends and confidantes of Chiang Kai-shek. The generalissimo who ruled all China, lost a civil war to the Communists, and retreated with his republican government to Taiwan intended the Grand Hotel to be his own version of the forbidden city: the imperial haven where commoners were not welcome.

It is too far from town to attract most business travellers, and perhaps too intimidating for most tourists. But to walk through its overwhelming red lobby, to sit in the glass-walled "Chinese Dining Room" (as opposed to the "Western Dining Room" across the way) is to feel how Taiwan's supreme ruler once lived.

Look out from the room to a vision of harmonious green: the hotel's landscaped ground, blending into the horizon's wooded hills. This imperial perspective makes it easy to imagine that this is the seat of power of an enormous domain, this is the only China: the other China, the enormous one across the Straits of Taiwan, is somehow to be controlled from this perch.

That was Chiang's conceit, in all the years his Kuomintang movement claimed to represent the rightful government of China—until that fateful day a quarter century ago when Richard Nixon ignored Taiwan's feelings and led his United States to make peace with the People's Republic of China (PRC).

Today, the rise of the PRC in the global economy draws a parade of democratic countries all too willing to overlook repression and an absence of democracy in the pursuit of profit. There is little doubt in the world's mind about where the real China lies. Yet Taiwan endures, trying to avoid the role of historical relic, insisting as its leaders do that it is the model on the mainland.

"The Kuomintang isn't the party it once was," says E. Craig Wilson, director of general relations in the Canadian Trade Office in Taiwan. "It is fully democratic. The institutions and traditions of democracy are firmly established in Taiwan."

Stripped of diplomatic recognition by most countries, including Canada, Taiwan takes a supremely practical approach. It has amassed the sort of economic clout that makes it difficult to ignore. Taiwan is a developed country, with per capita income at western levels and a high standard of education and health care for its twenty-one million people.

The economic success has built up one of the largest pools of investment capital in the world, with a surplus of $120 billion in Taiwan's foreign exchange reserves. Many countries court this capital, Canada included. But most importantly, it has allowed Taiwan to buy an insurance policy against the territorial ambitions of the People's Republic of China. While Taiwan is not officially allowed to invest in the PRC, Taiwanese officials privately concede they have invested some forty billion dollars in the PRC, mainly through intermediaries in Hong Kong.

"We have never maintained a two China policy," says Chang Shu-ti, a senior official in the Mainland Affairs Council. "We want to have a constructive dialogue" to reunite China as one country under a free and democratic government. Chang, like other Taiwanese officials, pours cold water on talk of outright Taiwanese independence. Taiwan represents a democratic alternative for all China, he says.

Last summer, China sent warships into the Taiwan Straits and staged invasion exercises on the mainland. It was a clear attempt to intimidate Taiwan, and required U.S. intervention to remove the threat. That move might have reflected internal politics in the PRC, says a leading political scientist, because in image terms, "it was a public relations fiasco for the mainland." In reality, both sides would like to maintain the status quo, says political scientist Ho Szu-yin, deputy director of the Institute of International Relations at Taipei's National Chengchi University.

Taiwan's goal of reuniting China under a free and democratic goal is "an ideal." Most people in the Taiwanese leadership "understand that it's not likely to happen, but they maintain the official position." That goal is essential to Taiwan's very survival, says Ho. If the movement for Taiwanese independence ever became serious, Taiwan's claim to represent the better way forward for all of China would be seriously undermined. Ho says it's "understandable" that countries like Canada would keep diplomatic relations with the PRC rather than Taiwan. "But we would hope our friends recognize that the two Chinas should resolve their status through dialogue, and by peaceful means."

An exiled city's vanished empire

Taipei, Republic of China, 9 November 1997

I n luminous French, one melodious syllable flowing into another, Béatrice is explaining the intricacy of a gossamer-thin ivory panel, so delicately filigreed it looks like a piece of woven silk. Her voice is a joy to the ears. After five days of hearing an American twang from just about every English speaker I've met in Taiwan, it's lovely to absorb Chinese culture in a language that's both soothing and engaging.

We are in the National Palace Museum on the outskirts of Taipei, home to the Imperial treasure Chiang Kai-shek "rescued" from Beijing's Forbidden City: first in the war with the Japanese, later from the civil war the Communists won. There is more gold than the mind can absorb, jade so lustrous it seems more a mirage than something real; here is pottery from 2500 B.C. decorated with swastikas. Between this display, and what remains in the Forbidden City, it is easy to be overwhelmed by the wealth and breadth of China's arts and treasures.

Meeting Béatrice—on a whim I had asked whether the museum had any francophone guides—is like the experience of Taipei itself: a welcome surprise. I hadn't expected Taipei to be so hilly, nor to find rain forest within minutes of the city core. Not even its most ardent residents would call Taipei pretty: it has all the sturdy functionality of a Canadian prairie city. The buildings are just what is needed, nothing more and nothing less. Take away the grand monuments to Chiang and Sun Yat-Sen, founder of the Chinese Republic, and there isn't even much that's ornamental. The city's architecture is much more utilitarian than decorative. Save the museum, there are few obvious attractions.

After a few days, the city starts to grow on you. In fact, Taipei is sort of like Edmonton. Few superficial charms, but a vibrant life beneath the first impressions. Before arriving here, my only impression of Taipei came from the subtext of Ang Lee's splendid film *Eat Drink Man Woman.* In Lee's vision, Taipei was a harsh, edgy sort of place, a little too driven for its own good. Certainly, being stuck in a traffic gridlock can reinforce that feeling. But the more time I spent walking, the better I liked the city. In fact, of the three Chinese cities I saw in a short span— Beijing, Hong Kong, and Taipei—it was Taipei that appeared the most authentically Chinese, at least in fulfilling my preconceptions of what China might be like.

Hong Kong is in a category by itself, a city that casts a spell I can't quite explain, drawing me back to its electric heart time upon time. Of the two rival Chinese capitals, Beijing and Taipei, it's Beijing that seems an artificial construct: a veneer of the global economy on an imperial city designed to overwhelm and intimidate any commoner who dares to approach.

Taipei, for all its choking traffic and boxy buildings, seems the most human and intimate of the three: gentler than the all-elbows rush of Hong Kong and much jollier than the mind-your-business survivalism of Beijing. Drive a few minutes out of Taipei, and you'll see hilltop pagodas, cemeteries going up hills, farm fields, rice paddies, prosperous villages. It's very much the China of my imagination, although it's far more affluent than one might think.

And within the city is the one thing that's rare in Beijing: children. Lots of children. At the Saturday flower market, stretching for blocks and blocks underneath a freeway, kids are everywhere. In strollers, in baby carriages, on backs, walking hand in hand with their parents. It's all so different from one-child-per-family Beijing, where parents seem nervous and too intensely attentive, caring for their one child as though she were as fragile as an egg. The most obviously Chinese characteristic of Taipei is the Betel nut stands. The reddish-brown spittle produced by betel and lime (the kind used in whitewash, not the fruit) was once the signature of the Orient. Now it's rarely seen outside South Asia, one of the many "old" habits frowned upon in the modernizing Asian countries.

In Taipei they chew the nut raw, rather than dried and chopped into a paan leaf as in India. The raw nut has the effect of an amphetamine. That's probably one explanation for why the late-night taxis are driven as though they were 747s trying to achieve takeoff speed.

On some stretches there seems to be a betel stand every few metres, with its trademark green neon. As the car crawls ahead, there is a surreal vision of jaws moving rhythmically in what seems like every other car, working up a buzz to deal with the traffic. I wonder what they would make of it in Singapore, where you are not even allowed to chew gum.

The Dalai Lama comes to Beijing

Beijing, China, 19 October 1997

"Time Flying!" declares the huge construction hoarding on Beijing's Wangfujiang (Palace Street), offering a pretty pastel portrait of an attractive young woman. Time is flying indeed.

Five years ago in the boomtown of Shenzhen, the hoardings featured an ardent Deng Xiaoping exhorting comrades to guard the revolution. In Beijing today, there are new exhortations: for Toshiba, BMW, new housing projects, Nortel, luxury condos, and, of course, McDonald's.

Communism is dead; capitalism lives. "Socialist market economy" becomes the mumbled catechism of a bygone faith, as China's ruling elite inspects the tres chic little suit in the Christian Dior boutique, or slips into the Beijing branch of that quintessential French department store, Galeries Lafayette.

The preferred vehicle these days is a Mercedes Benz. The bicycles are but a trickle now, confined to special bicycle lanes on the side of new expressways. For those who wish their consumption to be a little less conspicuous, there is the Santana, a Chinese-built version of a Volkswagen Passat.

The Lufthansa Centre is a chunk of the muscular new Deutschland plopped into the middle of Beijing: a Kempinski hotel, shopping arcades with prices to make a Canadian blanch, a jolly little braühaüs to enjoy a weisswürst and a draught, all run with a clockwork Germanic efficiency behind the Chinese faces and smiles.

The French and German presence is dwarfed by the real power in Beijing: the moneyed classes of Hong Kong. The din of construction, the astonishing mass of new projects, the cell phones, the crisply uniformed helpers in every shop and café, leads to a new understanding: On 1 July 1997, the People's Republic of China was absorbed by Hong Kong.

The end of British rule removed the last formal barrier to an economic colonization long in the making. Beijing is now part of Hong Kong, utterly transformed, soon to be a capital of skyscrapers and luxury hotels and shopping arcades, a fitting new symbol of what will soon become the world's largest economy.

"I liked it better the way it was," says a Vancouver lawyer who has lived in Beijing for seven years. "All this is brand new, it's almost impossible to recognize. Five years ago, there were only five thousand taxis in Beijing. Now there are eighty-five thousand."

Michael, whom I have hired to interpret for me, was born in the dying gasp of the Cultural Revolution. Now twenty-five, he credits the Communist party with enriching the lives of the Chinese people "because now, we can make so much money."

Out in the countryside, past the Great Wall, farmers haul cabbages on donkey carts; grubby-faced young women sell heaping baskets of persimmons on the roadside. Yet the lure of capitalism is changing their lives. At every single one of the many tourist destinations is an army of private stalls, as raucous as any free market you'll ever see, selling every kind of memento and toy imaginable.

Once upon a time, the Great Wall was built to keep the barbarians out. Its builders could not imagine one day the barbarians would come by sea, ascend the Pearl River, and sack the most glorious edifices of the Kingdom of Heaven. They arrived in 1860 at the Summer Palace of Qing Dynasty, smashed the porcelains, and carted away the gold. They set fire to the magnificent lakeside temples and villas. They were called the Anglo-French Expeditionary Force, led by Lord Elgin, but they included every barbarian tribe China would have wished to keep from its gates: Sikhs, Scots, Tamils, Welsh, Mahrattas, Irish, Punjabis, Bretons, Rajputs, Normans, Afghans, Occitans, Pathans, Provençals. The Dowager Empress Xixi rebuilt the palace in 1886, only to see it sacked again. And she built it one more time, until the entire Qing Dynasty collapsed the Boxer Rebellion.

Now, the barbarians are all over the Summer Palace. And the Great Wall. And wherever they go, there are many occasions for them and their tourist dollars to be parted.

All of this seems at times too much to comprehend, because there is still a police state at the heart of the newly capitalist People's Republic of China. You wonder if the balancing act can last, if the ruling elite can resist the pressure for political empowerment from a growing middle class.

Then comes the twist. Michael takes me to the Lama Temple, a haven of the very Tibetan Buddhism the Chinese have destroyed in Tibet. The place is packed, its fourteen shrines filled with worshippers praying fervently in an incense haze. People pray in Communist China? Yes, of course, explains Michael. During the "bad period" God was dead, but now God lives. And there is an empty throne awaiting the return of the Dalai Lama. "We are free now," he says. And as I try to talk to him about my belief that real freedom flows from democracy, he says: "Oh yes, the instability."

Jean-Baptiste Besse and the France that disappeared

Paris, France, 15 March 1998

E ven at the best of times it was not a door to catch the eye. A dili-
gent stroller would have to know just what she was looking for,
and where, to find this particular treasure of French culture. For the
casual passers-by climbing this cobbled medieval street in the heart of
Paris, there were more obvious attractions. The bulk of the Pantheon
atop the hill, the ancient church of St. Stephen of the Mountain, even
the imposing facade of the Polytechnic School are more natural draws
for the eye. For years, thousands were drawn to the now-empty storefront tucked away on the right of St. Genevieve Mountain Street. The
humble and the powerful, the connoisseurs and the drunkards, neighbours and visitors from afar, walked through the doors that are now
locked for good, looked in the windows now papered over. And unless
today's passers-by know what this had once been, what once lay behind
the For Sale placard, there would be little to be gleaned from the sign
that remains modestly mounted above the door: Jean-Baptiste Besse.

There is nothing to announce this was once the most eccentric and
remarkable wine store in France, and perhaps the world. His name may
never adorn the Pantheon, France's monument to its glorious dead. But
Jean-Baptiste Besse certainly deserves his place in the ranks of cultural

icons, a representative of a certain Frenchness that is vanishing under the weight of modernity.

Until he died last year, well into his nineties—he was at least eighty-two when I last saw him eleven years ago—Monsieur Besse presided over the single greatest collection of old wines and choice brandies in Paris.

You might never have known it to look at the store. The wines could hardly be seen. You wondered which rickety shelf would fall first under its burden of beans, cassoulet, soups, the whimsical stock of a neighbourhood convenience store. The first wines you saw were jugs of Prefontaine. Cheaper than water, it fuelled the days of the *clochards*—the street people who lived downhill on the quays and banks of the Seine, quaffing their red in magnificent gargoyle shade cast by the Basilica of Our Lady of Paris. Only after this evidence of Monsieur Besse's intensely democratic instincts would you begin to discern the treasures: the bottles presented almost as an afterthought along the tops of the shelves, or displayed in half-hidden racks beneath the precarious shelves of beans.

Presiding over it, sizing up every customer with an omniscient eye, stood the proprietor: a compact *paysan* from the Auvergne in a worker's blue smock and long apron, and the inevitable beret capping the frank expression and bright eyes. Those who did not pass his scrutiny were left to wander around the store until they left of boredom. Those who went so far as to give offence—a too-careless remark, a dull or foolish question—could expect to buy nothing, no matter that they had money. But for the thousands like me who were fortunate enough to win a welcoming nod from Monsieur Besse, all things were possible, especially after the second visit. For me it was more a school than a store, the place where I learned volumes about wine with every old vintage Monsieur Besse offered. He would descend into his cellars—five levels cut into the rock of the hillside—and emerge with forgotten vintages from remarkable years. As for the price, he would estimate what you could afford, and charge accordingly. "The importance is that the bottle should please you," he would say, and leave it at that.

In the earliest years of the wine education at Monsieur Besse's store, I was offered wines from the 1930s at the price of current vintages. "It is always a necessity to know the flavours of mature wine," he would agree. And when I celebrated my twenty-sixth birthday in Paris, it was Monsieur Besse who dug out a bottle of 1955 Chateau Talbot, my birth year, and insisted I take it at a fraction of its price. As he explained it, he was making a huge premium already on what he paid for it years ago, "and there are others who can pay more."

The neighbours said he worked right up to the end. The wine stock was sold off at auction, explained Madame, wife to Marcel, whose Vietnamese restaurant Saigon Latin lies downhill around the corner. "Monsieur Besse's child is in the theatre. There was no one left in the family to carry on. It's too bad, but that's the way it is sometimes."

Beating swords into Euro shares

Paris, France, 10 May 1998

W hen the single European currency, the Euro, became a reality last weekend, nearly every account shone a spotlight on the antics of French President Jacques Chirac, who was trying to upset the applecart by insisting his apples go on top. To me, it was final proof that the new Europe really works. If the worst dispute between France and Germany is about who should govern the new Central Bank of Europe, then surely it is a quarrel worth celebrating.

Not so long ago, within living memory for many German and French people, each were the other's implacable foe. It was an enmity that claimed millions of lives. To the French, Germany was "the beast that sleeps across the Rhine." So deep was the mistrust after the First World War that France built the modern-day equivalent of an impregnable barrier. The Maginot Line ran for 250 kilometres from Sedan to Wissembourg, a formidable defence with fifty large fortifications and hundreds of kilometres of connecting tunnels, all buried within hills and ridges. The Germans went around it, of course, and made short work of conquering France during the Second World War.

The point was not lost on the postwar leadership of France. Charles de Gaulle, the wartime commander of the free French, understood the only "Maginot Line" that would succeed would be a lasting peace in which the nations of Europe would work towards common goals. More than a peace treaty that humiliated the loser—the terms of the First World War peace brought the economic ruination that permitted a Hitler to rise in Germany—Europe needed to become a community of nations, a community of shared interests and purpose.

To do so, he began with a vital core—an intimate alliance between France and Germany, and the determination neither would go to war with the other, ever again. This was a visionary decision, one that took considerable courage. After all, war had defined the Franco-German relationship. From 1871, and the Paris Commune that defied the occupying Prussian Army, to 1941, when de Gaulle fled Paris with a promise to return victorious, German invasion posed the greatest and most pervasive threat to France. The German province of Elsass and the French province of Alsace—one and the same—changed owners with every twist of war.

The peace de Gaulle launched enabled the creation of today's European union. Now, the Euro sets the crown on de Gaulle's vision. It is in every sense an epochal event. In fact, European union is much more a celebratory achievement than the dry language of treaties could ever indicate. The Euro is not so much an artificial construct as a natural evolution. It is an advance that reflects an economic reality, rather than a radical idea far ahead of its time.

The very advent of the Euro forces Europeans to consider a question that could be ignored, so long as Europe was seen as an economic union alone: can you form common policies in every intimate aspect of economic life, without a similar convergence in political life?

And whatever the short-term denial, the long-term answer is that a common currency will lead to even closer political union. European countries will always keep a fig leaf of national boundaries, national flags, national legislatures, and national languages. Europe is already so borderless—at least among the elites—that national identity seems destined to become more a cultural expression than a political one. Indeed, cultural distinctions may be the only borders that remain within Europe. Catch a high-speed train at lunchtime in Paris, and you can be in Milan for supper—a journey inconceivable even in the 1970s.

National boundaries in effect reflect the traditional home of Europe's core cultures. Once the Euro comes, the political sovereignty of its member countries—the strong nation-state identities that led to two world wars—will fundamentally diminish, if not disappear.

That may be the greatest value of the Euro. By cementing economic integration, by requiring political convergence in fact if not in law, it becomes a guarantor of European peace. At the very least, it inoculates Europe against the forces and currents that have fuelled centuries of war. The Euro in effect closes the gate on a millennium of war, and begins the new millennium with an achievable dream of prosperity and peace. This is a momentous achievement in human history. The prospect of a Europe free of war changes the defining realities that have shaped the world. Colonialism, wars of conquest, the spread of essentially European fights into world wars—none of these is to be feared again. In its most vital sense, the Euro goes well beyond economics—it becomes a symbol of hope, of a world where cooperation can prevail over confrontation. And that is a gift for us all.

How the oldest rivalry ends

Paris, France, 26 April 1998

When a British prime minister gets a standing ovation from both the right and the left in France's National Assembly, you know France is on the verge of a monumental change. This revolution promises to be the most peaceable in French history—but revolution it is, impelled by the impending economic union of Western Europe, and the relentless advance of racist theories and policies from the extremes into the mainstream of French politics.

In its own way, May 1998 could be as epochal an event in French history as May 1968, when the prosperous generation of France's post-war young demanded a liberation from confining policies and traditions that bound France to a largely vanished past. After rioting students used them as impromptu missiles in May 1968, the cobblestones of Paris's St. Michael Boulevard were permanently sealed under a layer of asphalt.

This time there is no need to take such precautions. The demonstrations in Paris—virtually a daily occurrence this spring—have been peaceable. The causes come down to two—an exit from the economic crisis that has left nearly one in six French residents unemployed, and a popular uprising against the openly racist policies of the National Front and its leader Jean-Marie Le Pen.

Fighting racism with rhetoric is relatively easy. Even President Jacques Chirac joined the fray, as did virtually every mainstream politician. A handful of rightist politicians who sought electoral accommodations with the National Front after it gained a little over 15 per cent of the vote in regional elections were promptly expelled from their parties.

Mainstream politicians have rebutted, for now, the National Front's notion that expelling all immigrants will end unemployment by leaving plenty of jobs for the French—mainly by pointing out many "immigrants" were born in France and are in fact French (a point reinforced in the summer of 1998, when a French team of rainbow origins captured the World Cup of football).

Racism will not be quelled unless unemployment is solved. And there is a dawning recognition that a solution requires a fundamental change in the way France views itself and its place in the world. "I am seized by the quality of his ideas, by their vigour, and by his intelligence," Chirac gushed after British Prime Minister Tony Blair seduced the French parliament with a forty-five-minute speech delivered in flawless French. "He opens new directions, new possibilities."

French politicians look with admiration to Blair, whose Britain has an unemployment rate below 5 per cent, a surging economy, and an economic climate attractive enough to induce French people to leave France—all the while professing socialist principles of compassion and protection for the powerless. It is this apparently seamless blend of the traditional divides of France's left and right that makes Blair so appealing. But to embrace Blair's ideas, really a refinement of the Thatcherism that gave birth to a borderless world, France will have to change a tradition of state intervention in every aspect of economic life—a tradition upheld by both the right and the left.

France's model of intervention is called *dirigisme*, or giving direction. The state sets the economic directions and the goals that the private sector then pursues. There have been times in the history of the postwar Fifth Republic where right-wing governments have been comfortable with nationalized banks.

"If you lose your job, fall ill, or have any difficulty in this country," says a Canadian friend making a new life for herself in Paris, "you naturally expect the government will support you." It's an extension of France's revolutionary principle that government is for the people. Its purpose is to serve the individual and to meet the needs of citizens. The emerging global economy and France's leading role in shaping a single European currency are threatening that traditional role of the state.

A leisurely forty-minute stroll along the length of Paris's most fashionable street—the Avenue of the Elysian Fields, running from Harmony Plaza to the Arch of Triumph—reveals ample evidence of the global economy. Foreign brand names, foreign restaurants, foreign goods and shops are to be found in plenty along the tree-lined avenue, the showpiece of what Chirac dubs as the capital of the world.

While many of the products of the global economy are celebrated in Paris—everything from Cuban cigars to pop-culture mementoes from the United States—the deeper, less superficial consequences of globalization are forcing France to redefine itself. State subsidies, generous spending on social goals, extensive nets of social programs—these are all called into question by the new imperatives of competition among western democracies, driven by smaller governments that require citizens to do more for themselves.

Blair's apparent success in blending compassion with competitiveness—made easier by the fact that high employment brings less demand for social services—can seem baffling to politicians brought up to believe the state is the leading pillar of national life. It will be revolutionary indeed if a formula bred in Britain proves to be the salvation of France.

Why too much history begets blood

Edmonton, Alberta, 11 July 1994

Anyone who believes diplomacy can establish a lasting peace in Bosnia should spend forty-five minutes with Fradja Trifkovic. I did, and I'm still reeling. He is the most frightening man I have met.

Trifkovic is an emissary of the Bosnian Serb government in Pale. He is in Edmonton to complain about a Western propaganda campaign aimed against Serbs. The truth, according to him, is something else: it's everyone else's fault. The war? The ethnic cleansing? The shelling of civilians? The sieges? The cynical games that kept United Nations humanitarian convoys blocked for days? Yes, it's all someone or something else's fault, mostly history's. And it is the inability to rise above history that dooms the Balkans to a fatal cycle of bloodshed and retribution. The Bosnia war, indeed the entire civil war in the former Yugoslavia, is the final chapter of the Second World War. The Great War brought the genocidal slaughter of Serbs at the hands of a fascist Croat state.

Those hatreds were frozen in time, never resolved. These on top of the dormant volcano that is the Balkans, with its terrible history of conquest and rule, and the centuries-long Turkish occupation that brought Islam to the lands of the southern Slavs. For Trifkovic this history seems to be a living reality. Serbs are history's victims, and yes it is always another's fault. Yugoslavia was an artificial construct, designed to deny Serbs their rights, says Trifkovic. So that's Tito's fault. The notion of a multiethnic Bosnia is an absurdity, because it never existed. It was part of Yugoslavia, so Bosnia too is a mistake.

And mistakes must be corrected. As soon as the Serbs' rightful territorial claim was disputed, as soon as the first shot was fired, "we knew there would be a paroxysm of blood that would claim a million lives." He says this in an even tone, with a bland expression—not the Serbs' fault, you see. Besides, it's made to sound worse by the western media, by reporters like the *Guardian's* Maggie O'Kane and the *New York Times's* John Burns, who told lies to win the Pulitzer Prize. "After you win the Pulitzer," says Trifkovic, "you can't very well admit you're lying, can you?"

Maybe it's the fact he doesn't raise his voice. Maybe it's because he speaks in an offhand way, with a trace of upper crust Britain in his accent. Whatever it is, I'm much more able to comprehend gun-toting barbarians or excitable lunatics. I just can't understand how an educated man—a scholar of history and political science—can so quietly and casually justify the most appalling brutality. It would be different, perhaps even easier to accept, if he were seething with hatred. But he's far too calm for that. I have never heard evil expressed in such cultured tones.

Nothing we take as normal or human is possible in Bosnia, Trifkovic says. It is a "politically correct fantasy" to imagine Bosnians of different backgrounds can live together. The images of the Sarajevo Olympics? All make-believe. The fact Serbs and Muslims are intermarried? An aberration. The fact a third of the soldiers in the Muslim-led Bosnian army are Serbs? Forced conscription. That they are officers? Only one is a high commander.

These are all exceptions to the rule—Serbs need their own space, their own identity, free of Muslims, in order to flourish. Perhaps Trifkovic has a sense of irony, for he stops short of using the term *lebensraum*. Trifkovic predicts the failure of the latest Bosnian peace plan. It is another Western trick, designed to make the Serbs look like villains.

What's the problem? It's all very involved, about which corridor is linked up where. But in essence it is this: it would preserve, geographically, the illusion of a multiethnic Bosnian state. And that the Serbs cannot have. That just does not reflect the reality of Bosnia, he says.

The same goes for the partition of Sarajevo. The partition of Sarajevo? Oh yes, says Trifkovic. You mean a formal division of the city? Oh no, nothing that crude. It would be a Serb city, and the Muslims would exist at their grace. Muslims could have "safe" passage in and out of Sarajevo, under the watch of Serb guns in the hills.

Against all this there is an image that will not recede, an image of delight. It was during Universiade 83, the World University Games in Edmonton: at a local mall, Yugoslav folk dancers were showing their steps two by two. The announcer, a fellow with the genial demeanour of a fond uncle, would announce the names with pride: Skopje, Belgrade, Sarajevo, Split, and Zagreb. They were beautiful, these men and women, in the way of figures in classical paintings. Bright eyes, smiles that lit up their faces, intimate glances from one to the other: love was definitely in the air.

Ever since this war began, I have wondered what became of them, of those young dancers so consumed with joy on a faraway Edmonton afternoon. I cannot believe, dare not believe that their tender feelings were transmuted into hate. Against the reality of Trifkovic and the mentality he represents, what chance is there for normal human emotions to flourish?

Why loving the forsaken brings joy

Cochin, India, 24 September 1996

Vijayamma's day begins at 5:30 A.M. in her large, spotless bunga-low, when she puts on a pot of coffee for her older children and wakes them. By 6 A.M., all thirteen of her children are up, brushing their teeth, having a wash or a quick bath. The ones who need help with schoolwork leave for tutoring, and Vijayamma begins cooking brunch for the family. The kids leave for school by 8:45 A.M., eating a hot breakfast of rice and lentils and vegetables, packing a snack for midday. That leaves Vijayamma with three-year-old Malu and thirteen-month-old Ponnu. She'll put the girls to play by the indoor sandbox, spreading out toys and puzzles. Her house is designed so she can watch them while she works.

This is a taxing routine for any mother, but Vijayamma is an excep-tional woman. "At first, I didn't know if I could look after so many chil-dren properly, but now I'm used to it," she says in her native Malayalam, the language of India's southern Kerala state. "I'd like to have even more children." When Malu is three and a half, she'll go to play school, just a few steps outside the house. By then Vijayamma will be ready to raise a new baby, a baby someone else threw away. All the children in her house are hers, yet she gave birth to none of them.

Vijayamma is a mother at the SOS Children's Village in the lush Kerala countryside, just outside the ancient port city of Cochin. The SOS villages began in Austria just after the Second World War, when the late Dr. Hermann Gmeiner thought abandoned children needed a mother rather than an orphanage. "A mother is the primary need for every child, irrespective of nationality, creed, political beliefs or ideology," Gmeiner wrote.

That notion fits perfectly into Indian culture, where the role of the mother is revered, where until a generation ago children grew up in a joint family, with lots of cousins. Put destitute children in a new family, and they'll grow up with love, Gneimer believed. That's put into practice in 125 countries, in 343 SOS Children's Villages.

The one in Cochin is one of thirty-two in India—places of compassion amid the misery and cruelty that fills so many children's lives. Vijayamma is one of fifteen mothers in the Cochin village, each with their own house, raising anywhere between ten and fifteen children—children discarded by their birth parents.

Malu's birth mother left her on a bus when the baby was a day old—she asked the woman in the next seat to hold her for a minute, and never came back. Ponnu was a premature baby; her parents abandoned her in the hospital.

To step into Vijayamma's home is to know this is a place full of love. The older children help look after the younger ones. Even so, it's hard to imagine Vijayamma can cope with so many. "I never get angry with them, never!" she exclaims. "In other homes, there are parents, grandparents, aunts and uncles to give the children love. Here, there is only me. If I don't give them love, no one else will."

As we talk, Ponnu climbs on Vijayamma's lap with attention getting cries of "Amma" (mother) and tries to dislodge Malu, who's absolutely entrenched on her mother. Fifteen-year-old Mini, home on holidays from a boarding school for bright students, whisks Ponnu away to play.

The SOS children in Cochin go to play school on the premises, then to schools in nearby communities. Vijayamma has four gifted children who are top academic performers. Once SOS kids reach high school age, boarding schools become an option, especially for high achievers. Boys usually leave their mothers at sixteen to live in SOS youth hostels. At twenty-one, boys are encouraged to make their own way in the world; girls can stay longer in the SOS system, until they're well established in life.

SOS children are taught they're special. Besides their mothers, they have resident nurses and counsellors to look after them, to help them cope with the rejection and discrimination they sometimes encounter at school and elsewhere. In its essence, SOS is a chance at life for children discarded even as their lives began. For the mothers, SOS work is a commitment of compassion and love.

Vijayamma was widowed in her twenties. Rather than remarry as her parents wished, she applied to the SOS home in Cochin when it opened in 1988. After a rigorous selection—three interviews and many opportunities to back out—she made a lifelong commitment. Now thirty-five, she will take in new babies until she's 45forty-five and "retire" when the last is grown up. In the SOS system, retirement means a home in the village of her choice, a pension, and a commitment that all her needs will be looked after.

"I've raised five babies from the time they were newborns, starting with this one," she says, giving eight year old Shalini a hug. Vijayamma has nine daughters and four sons—many more girls than boys are abandoned in India.

SOS villages are financed by sponsorships from the local community and from abroad. In India, it usually costs thirty-five dollars Cdn to cover a child's needs for a month. Vijayamma gets a monthly budget to maintain her kids. A truck delivers fresh vegetables, fruit, and groceries to the village store every day. When she needs a break, she can get someone else to come in and cook, twice a week. And when she goes on holidays, she'll take her three or four youngest children with her, leaving the others in the care of a nanny.

Children at the Cochin village are raised in one of Kerala's three major faiths—Christianity (established by St. Thomas in the fifty-second year of the Christian era), Hinduism, and Islam. If a child's religion is unknown—often the case—SOS administrators will choose one at random, says village director Titus Poovakulam. In India, religion is as much a matter of culture as belief. In the SOS village, kids grow up mingling with children of every tradition, in Christian homes next to Hindu and Muslim homes. Each evening, there's a fifteen-minute universal prayer service that unites all three faith traditions.

Education in India is highly competitive. The moms help as much as they can with the homework, but there are tutors available in the evening to help with English and advanced subjects. There are no televisions in the homes; children can go to the village's common TV area only with their tutors' permission, after all their homework is done.

At home in the evening, Vijayamma makes a point of spending some time with each of her children, before tucking them into one of the three bedrooms. The youngest ones will sleep with her. When Ponnu arrived, Malu cried bitterly for two days, and asked Amma to send the baby away. But now, Vijayamma says with an optimistic smile as Malu clings to her fiercely, "she has really learned to love the little one."

An Ugly Indian's fishy fish story

Mumbai, India, 14 September 1996

For maybe the third time in my life, I wanted to hit somebody. The guy was so brutal, so primitive, that reason and persuasion wouldn't do. He dealt in raw power, and the arrogance of newfound wealth. And he was busy exercising it on a hapless waiter who would almost certainly lose his job.

It all started over a fish. I was at the Ming Palace, a comfortable Chinese restaurant with middle-class prices. There are dozens of nicely appointed air-conditioned restaurants like it in Mumbai (formerly Bombay), India's financial capital and home to at least twelve million people. Next to me was a table of twenty, evidently three thirtyish brothers, their families, and some friends.

Having nearly finished their meal, they decided they were still hungry. Their leader, a moustached type in an elegant silk shirt, asked the waiter what else he could recommend. "The fish." "How long would it take?" "Not long, maybe five or ten minutes." When a little more than ten minutes passed, the waiter was summoned. "Cancel the order," said the leader, "your ten minutes are up." "Sorry," said the waiter, "it's coming out of the kitchen just now." "Forget it," said Silk Shirt, "you're late." The next fifteen minutes produced an utterly obnoxious performance, including the summoning of the manager and the restaurant owner. Silk Shirt lectured them on the oral contract implicit in promising a fish in five minutes. He would accept no apology, and of course, he would not accept the fish. Moreover, he told his family between the summoning of senior management; "these people actually have the brass to ask us to pay for the meal."

There was an undercurrent of racial tension between the Indian diners and the Chinese waiters and managers. But more than anything, it was the absolute display of power. The Ming Palace had lost his business forever, said Silk Shirt. How dare they demand payment? It was at this point, my appetite completely lost, I felt like smacking the guy. Of course, Canadian caution prevailed. I said nothing, and I still feel ashamed I held my peace.

It's been a long time since I've had such a visceral reaction. But Mumbai brought it out in me. It's a place where money counts for everything. Before Mumbai, I'd seen this attitude in only two other cities, New York and Hong Kong. In Mumbai, the skewed housing market makes the disparity worse. Rent control laws mean rents are fixed once set; the last revision was in 1968. Areas that might be redeveloped for housing are left to languish. The new housing that goes up is prohibitive.

Middle managers in companies, and government employees, get company or government housing. But the open market is brutal. On Cuffe Parade, a boulevard running along a peninsula in Mumbai harbour, there are perhaps fifty high-rise apartment buildings full of million-dollar suites.

This means a lot of people with ordinary jobs—retail clerks, secretaries, waiters, sales personnel—either live in slums or eight to a room in rented accommodation. These circumstances breed a clear social division —the owners, and the rest. And the attitude of Mumbai's owners is just the same as those who live in Hong Kong's Mid-Levels, or Manhattan's Upper East Side. Some of them seem to gain a special pleasure in denigrating the serving or (as they would see it) servant classes.

It was reinforced another night at the Bombay Brasserie, a popular restaurant where the diners' scorn for the waiters was palpable. I saw it in shops, in the utter indifference of those driving to those walking, a prevalent sense that those without money were of no account.

In five weeks of travelling all over India, Mumbai was the only place where the arrogance of wealth was so heavily felt. In other places—notably Coimbatore where the industrialists donate schools and hospitals to the community—there was a sense of obligation to the community, of a responsibility to someone other than themselves.

Mumbai showed me the face of selfishness and greed, of individual well-being overtaking any concern for the common good. It showed what could happen when a few people have an elite life, with everyone else existing to serve them. And it made me think of home, of the chronic unemployment in Canada, of the skilled people who are under-employed, of the university graduates waiting on tables, the hardening of attitudes, the hostility towards those on public assistance, the notion social programs and universal Medicare are a frill and a luxury. These are the germs of the Mumbai disease.

I hope Canadians' sense of compassion will be strong enough to resist: the alternative really is unthinkable.

How Savonarola was reborn in the United States

Edmonton, Alberta, 11 October 1998

I t's unfair to compare Kenneth Starr to Joseph McCarthy. The parallel
is leaping to the mind of some U.S. commentators who are rightly
aghast at the prosecutor's zeal of the former judge hired to investigate
alleged misdeeds by U.S. President Bill Clinton. They seize on the fact
that Starr, in a report full of the most revolting detail of a private dal-
liance, omitted a key line of testimony: Monica Lewinsky's unequivocal
statement that no one ever asked her to lie or offered her a job in
exchange for her silence regarding her affair with Clinton.

Yet the comparison to McCarthy is highly unfair, despite some similarities. McCarthy, the alcoholic Wisconsin senator who led a witch-
hunt of alleged Communists in the United States in the 1950s, was
indeed consumed by the sort of zeal Starr displays. Like Starr, he was a
lawyer and circuit court judge. He too displayed willingness to wreck
careers and destroy reputations on the flimsiest of evidence.

It may be an easy comparison for some, because McCarthy's House
Un-American Activities Committee also used the police-state tactics evident in Starr's abduction of Lewinsky. As we now know, the young
woman was on her way to meet her "friend" Linda Tripp for lunch at a
pleasant hotel, only to see Tripp signal FBI agents who snatched Lewinsky

and took her away. The FBI and Starr's team of prosecutors did not inform Lewinsky of her constitutional rights. They threatened her with twenty-seven years in jail—for allegedly lying in a civil suit! They would not let her call a lawyer, which should have been her inviolate right. When she cried for her mother, they sneered at her. And all to do what? To induce her to entrap the president of the United States, to "prove" that he too may have lied in a politically motivated civil suit later thrown out by a Republican judge because it proved to be a load of rubbish.

And on this madness, partisan legislators are prepared to destroy a presidency! No wonder German Chancellor Helmut Kohl says the whole thing makes him vomit. No wonder world leaders gave Clinton a standing ovation at the United Nations. No wonder Czech President Vaclav Havel—whose own history of infidelity does not bear scrutiny—stood sympathetically at Clinton's side. No wonder South African President Nelson Mandela declared: "Our morality does not permit us to abandon our friends."

Who can comprehend this Starr-struck madness, outside the U.S. right wing and its handful of purring Boswells in British and Canadian media? Yes, it's easy to see why some of the few sane people left in the U.S. media are evoking visions of the Communist witch-hunt. Despite these similarities, it is still wrong to say Starr is like McCarthy. Because like it or not, agree with him or not, McCarthy could at least claim a basis for his conduct. There was indeed a Cold War, and it wasn't entirely unreasonable to think some Americans in high places were in the employ of the Soviet Union. McCarthy may have been a paranoid zealot, but the communism he so egregiously pursued did in fact challenge American interests. Starr can claim no such justification. Which is why it's terribly unfair to McCarthy's memory to link his name with Starr's. But Starr's pursuit of Clinton's immoral conduct does have a historical precedent.

There was a time when a mighty republic fell under the spell of a moral zealot. He too was consumed with rooting out vice. He saw sin and corruption everywhere, particularly on the part of the eminent figures of the day. He thought it his divine duty to root out sin, to establish a Christian republic of perfection and virtue. He rejected all calls to act reasonably, spurned all attempts at conciliation. He felt he was on a righteous mission, his interpretation of his duty was holier than anyone else's.

His name was Girolamo Savonarola. He began by attacking the influential Medici family in 1490s Florence, and ended up denouncing Pope Alexander VI. When the Florentines had had enough, they put the Dominican monk on trial for heresy and sedition. Savonarola was excommunicated. He and two of his fellow prosecutors were hanged, then burned at the stake—just as Savonarola himself had "cleansed" sinners by the purification of fire. Those momentous events of 1498 Florence are reflected in the United States of 1998. On the five hundredth anniversary of Savonarola's execution, his memory is revived in the crusade of Kenneth Starr.

Florentines knew Savonarola was right about the immorality and sin. But they recoiled because he made no concession for human frailty, because the purity of conduct Savonarola demanded was singularly lacking in the powerful humans of the day, let alone the lesser mortal. As they meet to impeach Clinton for his sexual misdeeds, I sincerely hope the members of the United States Congress read and understand history.

She saw the face of God in everyone

Calcutta, India, 14 September 1997

> Too long a sacrifice
> Can make a stone of the heart.
> O when may it suffice?
> —WILLIAM BUTLER YEATS, EASTER 1916

For the future Saint Teresa of Calcutta, the answer was "never." What lesser humans saw as sacrifice was for her the essence of love. When the hearts of others were made stone, when hardened faces turned away from the flotsam and jetsam of the human race, Mother Teresa bent down and gave wing to the fallen.

Where so many of us saw destitution and despair, Mother found the animating force of the universe, what she described as the face of God. She saw more clearly than anyone did the bright spark of the divine in every human being. She put into heartfelt practice Christ's credo of unconditional love, and showed us compassion is the noblest human virtue. Mother's remarkable life was built on the selfless and incessant application of caritas in its fullest sense. She was for many a living Mater Misericordiae; all the good she did lives on in the thousands of women and men who have pledged their own lives to carrying on what she began.

She was one woman. Just one woman. From the power of her soul, from the force of her will, from the inexhaustible well of her mercy, she showed the world there is worth in every human life, human dignity is a Divine endowment that should remain inviolate.

> . . . and the city was sinking and on the stone pavement
> the Nazarene showed you his heart,
> what were you looking for?
> —GEORGE SEFERIS, MYTHISTORIMA, POEM 13

For what no one else would seek, Mother might have replied. The ecstasy of tending a leper's wounds, the bliss of cleaning the filth from the enfeebled and abandoned who lay down to die by the side of the road, the joy of loving the unloved. Not far from her shelter is a temple dedicated to another mother Calcuttans revere: Kali, the Divine, represented as the eternal power of time. When the devout in Mother Teresa's adopted city think of God, they think of an all-powerful mother. That's why it was so easy for so many to see in Mother Teresa an aspect of the Universal Mother celebrated in pre-Christian faiths (and in early Christianity, for all we know).

Humankind's earliest civilizations felt a need to revere the image of a divine mother who was the fount and store of all hope, the embodiment of all women in the universe, the personification of all mothers. She is worshipped as the divine intelligence in the heart of all living creatures, the auspicious Mother from whom blessings are sought. She is the compassionate Mother, the remover of sorrows, the One who offers shelter and refuge, the saviour and the redeemer.

> Mother, I shall weave a chain of pearls for thy neck
> with my tears . . . The stars wrought anklets of
> light to adorn thy feet, but mine will hang upon
> thy breast. This my sorrow is absolutely mine own,
> and when I bring it to thee as my offering thou
> rewardest me with thy grace.
> —RABINDRANATH TAGORE, GITANJALI, POEM 83

It can be so hard to discern the face of evil. When a murderer is caught, when a rapist is convicted, we wonder how someone who looks so bland and ordinary can be capable of the most bestial acts. It can be even more difficult to discern the face of indifference. It so often lurks behind the adored and beautiful mask of celebrity.

We frequently hear of the success of Hollywood's latest twenty-million-dollarstars; we hardly ever hear they have used the power wealth confers in the service of the suffering. Is it ever difficult to discern the face of the truly good? Of those whose radiance comes from the abiding presence of love? Tens of thousands of the rejected felt the love of Mother's hands, knew the grace of Mother's touch, heard the soothing lilt of her Bengali as she calmed them towards what might be their final sleep. They came to her embrace one by one and escaped that worst of human fates: to die unknown and alone. With a dazzling clarity, Mother helped us to see: Love heals. Love nourishes. Love overcomes. Love costs nothing to give. If we so wish, each of us can follow Mother's path in our own way, in our own measure. Our steps may be small, the beginning might be modest, and there is no assurance we can ever find another Mother Teresa in our midst. If we dare to unleash the power of love, we may find a life of meaning and purpose and within it the beginnings of our own fulfillment.

How India finally spent money on the poor

Bangalore and New Delhi, India, September 1996

I t was either a supreme acting job, or a moment of genuine emotion. His voice breaking, seemingly on the verge of tears, Prime Minister Harahanahalli Doddegowda Deve Gowda recalled his last conversation with his mother, who died shortly after he assumed the nation's most responsible office. "She told me to do something for the poor," he told the huge outdoor rally in Bangalore, the capital city of his home state of Karnataka. And with that came an announcement no prime minister had dared make before—not even in the heyday of the planned economy. In the next five years, said Deve Gowda, education would become a fundamental right for all children up to the age of fourteen—it would be "free and compulsory." In a country where millions of children work, where the basics of childhood are denied to many, this has revolutionary implications. But he wasn't finished.

By 2000, he said, villages in India—where 75 per cent of the population lives—would have safe drinking water. There would be free primary health care centres for every Indian. All poor families without shelter would get some form of public housing, or assistance with housing. Every village in India would become accessible by road. Every school child would get a midday meal. This is an immense agenda to fill in only three years. Deve Gowda hopes to do so by harnessing the fruits of a freer economy and foreign investment to provide jobs and growth.

Dr. Manmohan Singh, who is soon to receive an honorary degree from the University of Alberta, launched India's economic reforms five years ago. The fruits of this economic liberalization have brought an exponential growth in the middle class—and an overwhelming demand for electric power, good roads, and state-of-the-art communications.

India's economy is growing at 7 per cent a year after inflation. If that growth rate can be sustained—and Finance Minister P. Chidambaram believes it can be—India will be a developed country by 2020. Chidambaram's 2020 plan implies people who are now considered poor would have access to quality education and health care, to clean water, to decent jobs. Critics do not believe it can be easily achieved. "The welfare of the poor supposedly occupies centre stage in this budget," says Yashwant Sinha of the opposition Bharatiya Janata Party, a former finance minister. "I think it is absolutely incorrect to say that; there is nothing here for the poor."

Social spending has barely increased, says Sinha. Madhu Dandavate of the Janata Dal, another former finance minister, says the government's hands are tied by "a number of serious constraints" including a budget deficit around 6 per cent of national income, and interest payments on India's external debt. Yet Deve Gowda, the first Indian prime minister from a lower caste, is looking beyond the narrow analyses of economists to the fundamental challenge of ensuring India becomes a more equitable country. His thirteen-party United Front government, a coalition that includes Marxists and centrists, represents a broader governing consensus than any India has seen.

So far, the benefits of the last five years of economic liberalization have helped only a minority. The lives of most Indians have yet to improve. People who once struggled to survive might have enough money now to buy stereos, televisions, and even motorbikes. But if they live in one of India's big cities, especially Mumbai (formerly Bombay), they most likely live in a slum. "The question isn't whether you can buy consumer goods, it's what kind of life you can buy with your money," says Dr. Sushmita Ghosh, a California-trained economist working with Citibank in Madras. "If you can't acquire decent housing, if you don't have basic sanitation, what does it matter that you can buy a television?"

Rural dwellers, too, might have access to more money as crops and productivity improve. Many villages lack clean water and basic health care. In the villages, though, people with land at least have a place to live and eat. The same can't be said of the big cities. Even in the capital New Delhi, there is more slum housing than safe low-income housing, although this is beginning to change.

In Mumbai, there's no low-income housing for people who work in the private sector—most workers are in small businesses and factories. Everywhere you turn is a glaring contrast between high-rise apartment blocks—where a two-bedroom suite can cost one million dollars U.S. in a neighbourhood like Cuffe Parade or Malabar Hill—with waves of slum housing lapping at their foundations. Any warm evening with a breeze carries a lingering odour of human excrement—few slum dwellings have plumbing, and public toilets are few and far between. Built as squatters' camps, the Mumbai slums are now legal. The city spends little in trying to provide basic services to the millions who live there.

The situation isn't as dire elsewhere in India. In other cities, there's investment in rebuilding slum areas as viable housing; municipal services are finally reaching the poorest of the poor. In New Delhi, for instance, much of the land once occupied by squatters has been legalized, and people who once had slum shanties are able to use their recently acquired savings to build permanent dwellings.

If the economy continues to surge, it's possible to see Deve Gowda's ambitious plan taking shape more quickly than critics imagine. If the economy takes a tumble, his promises will be more difficult to keep. The prime minister is determined to find the money, one way or the other— the clean water promise alone will cost $2.5 billion.

With an economy that grew by 7 per cent after inflation last year, Deve Gowda can reasonably expect robust revenues. The real question is whether he'll have a free hand to invest those revenues in basic human needs before the interests of other more powerful groups prevail.

Gowda and Chidambaram are gambling they can keep everyone happy—and indeed, Chidamabaram's budget was remarkable in drawing praise from nearly everyone. If economics ever squeezes the country again, it's difficult to imagine that the prime minister will be able to put the interests of the poor first. There are too many demands from the newly rich and the traditional rich, and Deve Gowda's minority government is in a race against time. If his government survives, if its reforms survive, the remaking of India will at last be at hand.

How India's capitalists show
a human face
Coimbatore, India, September 1996

I f there really is such a thing as capitalism with a human face,
Coimbatore is the place to find it. A city of a million people at the
base of the Nilgiri Hills in the southern state of Tamil Nadu,
Coimbatore bills itself as India's "centre of techcellence." Coimbatore's
business houses build schools, hospitals, and community centres. "It's
our pleasure to give something back to our community," says Dr. G.S.
Keshavamurthy, managing director of SIV Industries. To him and his colleagues, it makes perfect business sense to invest in a better quality of life
for their employees and fellow citizens.

Besides, says industrialist K.G. Balakrishnan; it's better than giving
money to a corrupt government. His KG group of companies donated a
220-bed speciality hospital and five schools that educate twenty-two
hundred students. "We're very nauseated by the corruption of both the
central and the state governments," he says. What's the use of giving tax
money to politicians who'll steal it? He would much rather spend his tax
money directly on things that develop the community. Besides the
schools, he covered the entire cost of building a new mosque and a new
Hindu temple in Coimbatore. The new government in Tamil Nadu
state is trying to stamp out corruption, but Balakrishnan says it may be

an impossible task. His family-run companies—five brothers and two brothers-in-law run businesses as diverse as cotton ginning, engineering, financial service, and entertainment complexes—have to make payoffs at every turn. Balakrishnan—he has been known to unnerve telephone callers by answering "Hello, KGB"—says the system is so pervasive it can grind down any clean politician intent on reforms.

As managing director of KG Denim, he exports forty to fifty container loads every month. Balakrishnan, who makes ten million metres of denim a year for clients like Wrangler, Pepe, Lee Cooper and Moustache, can't afford any delays in a shipment. And for each container, he has to pay one thousand rupees (forty dollars) on the side to a government official. If he didn't, every single bundle of denim in every container would be subject to inspection. The official would painstakingly unpack every container, simply to verify shipment contents. The official has made it clear it would take at least a fortnight to "inspect" every container. The amount may not seem like much, but consider that five thousand to seven thousand rupees a month is a good middle class salary.

Most companies, no matter how they complain about government, get on with the business of finding a competitive edge. It's a typical attitude in Coimbatore, a city built by migrants attracted to the pleasant high-altitude climate. "Next to Bangalore, we have the best weather in India," says alloys manufacturer S.N. Varadarajan. Now, they're creating an economic climate that encourages innovation.

Cotton mill owner D. Lakshminarayanaswamy invests in designer seeds that will enable cotton growers to increase crop yield by up to 60 per cent. "We have the largest acreage of cotton in the world, but not the largest production," he says. Farmers usually get two crops a year; Lakshminarayanaswamy urges them to grow high-yield cotton in the four months between rice crops. "It may serve our self-interest, but the farmer also benefits," he says.

Coimbatore's industrial development means "there is no unemployment here," says Balakrishnan. It might seem an extravagant claim, given that job shortages are endemic in other cities—poor people take what work they can to survive, while educated graduates sit idle looking for a "suitable" job. In Coimbatore, the industries absorb thousands of skilled people every year. Coimbatore's industrialists scour the world for the best technology they can find. Intelligent use of capital means nearly every establishment has the most modern equipment money can buy—freeing workers for less monotonous tasks.

"Our labour costs are so low that we will always employ a larger number of people," says Lakshminarayanaswamy, managing director of Sri Ramakrishna Mills and chair of the Indian Cotton Mills Federation. But the people are employed in making sure there are no breakdowns on the banks of power looms that spin cotton, polyester, and viscose into yarn. A lot more people are employed in quality control, in packaging and shipping, in customer relations.

R. Doraiswamy's Salzer group "makes the most of technology and of our people," he says. At one of the mills, computer-driven machines churn out thousands of metres of intricate embroidery. The women who walk up and down the line looking for thread breaks would have had a very different job a generation ago. Then, an embroidery factory would have meant women turning out embroidery pieces by hand for a pittance. Now designs are done on a computer, which calibrates the needles for the pattern. The only unskilled manual work is in cutting patches of embroidery out of the cloth. This is the lowest paid work at the plant—about fifty rupees a shift—and it attracts a lot of migrant workers who might otherwise be out in the sun breaking rocks, clearing vegetation, or carrying loads at construction sites.

Most jobs in the factories require a sound technical education—gained at polytechnics that typically offer three-year diplomas. At Salzer's electrical components company, a joint venture with Plitron of Mississauga, Ontario, the majority of employees are women, all of them diploma holders. The demand for women technicians is especially strong in the Coimbatore area, says Narayan Jayabal, a Canadian engineer who now directs the joint venture. "When it comes to detailed assembly, or checking quality, we find that women are much better. The guys just don't have that kind of commitment," says Jayabal. "We put them to work on the moulds, the lathes, and the heavy equipment."

Balakrishnan believes Coimbatore can set a standard for India in the use of technology and in developing a competitive advantage—all that's holding it back is corruption. "If the system doesn't change," he says with at least a hint of seriousness, "then Coimbatore should declare itself independent from India."

How I came to lose my river

Midnapore District, India, 21 June 1998

In the tinted recollection of a happy childhood, it stands out as the perfect river.

Neither the grandest, nor the most significant, just a river that was as it should be: expansive shallows, broad sandbars, and the lure of treacherous water in midstream—what more did anyone need?

In the mornings, just before the heat climbed into your skin, a brisk walk along the hard-packed dirt paths of the village—bamboo groves and thorn fences around earthen-walled thatch houses, pumpkin and cucumber vines spreading across the roofs—led to the nearest *ghat*. Sometimes, bare feet would squish berries or fruit shed by the overhanging trees and a weary adult face might light up at the sight of children running by. A quick plunge into the water would wash away the last tendrils of sleep, and there you would play until someone was sent to fetch you home.

The river was called The Golden Ribbon—*Subarnarekha*, in the Sanskrit of that long-forgotten age when human civilization was new and people knew the magic and mystery of naming all that was unnamed in the world. It was the also the ribbon of a joyous abandon in all the holidays I spent in my mother's village, and the ribbon that binds me to my earliest memories. I grew up by that river: when my parents were off in Britain earning graduate degrees and on every precious holiday after they returned. The river and the village were a world of their own, with a sense of timelessness, untouched by the swirl of a turbulent history. The river ghat was the place where we arrived and departed, on every holiday.

If the water was low, we would cross by ox-cart. Lying on the straw in the cart-bed, shaded by a cover of woven bamboo, I would look down from the cart and watch the water go by, just below my face. In high water, we would cross by hand-hewn boat. The ferry was sturdy enough to carry at least a dozen people and their belongings, and the boatmen would point out exactly where the treacherous currents swirled.

After a particularly hot crossing, someone might split open an enormous watermelon right off the vine. And the rickshaw-pedallers waiting to take us the final few kilometres to the railway station at Dantan would catch the few extra minutes in the shade.

It was a river, a road, and a life for all that lived along it. We would cross around the place where the river began to spread into a delta, an incredibly fertile place that provided all the necessities. The boatmen spoke of the muddy surge of the monsoon-fed stream into the Bay of Bengal, about twenty-five kilometres downstream from their ferry ghats.

The village died for me with my grandparents, and I haven't been back in twenty years—there's no one to go back to, only the memory of a place as it once was, of a time as it once was, when the world was simpler. No return could bring back the simple joy of that first plunge into the water of every childhood summer. But even if I wanted to, it would now be impossible for me to make the journey I always longed to— joining the boatmen on a leisurely float to where the river meets the sea. I can't, because ordinary people aren't allowed there any more. That rich delta, those villages on the mouth of the Subarnarekha are off limits now. The Indian government appropriated them in the early 1980s, the people moved off, haphazardly compensated for the loss of their home and their lands.

The place where the rich alluvial soil fed and enriched tens of thousands of people is now part of India's main missile testing range. It is the place where Indian scientists test rockets capable of carrying nuclear warheads deep into the heart of China. This is how innocence passes, how a timeless place is thrust into the ugliest aspects of modernity.

One generation you're growing fruit and vegetables, the next you're watching missiles roar over what had once been your land. And if the calamity of nuclear war ever comes to pass, will anyone pushing the buttons know or care what that water used to feel like on an eight-year-old's face?

After all is said and done, after all the convictions are aired, after the evil of nuclear weapons is laid bare for all to see, a decision can come down to the simplest things. I can give you all of my logical constructs against nuclear weapons, argue with intellect and passion for disarmament, tell you why you should support Abolition 2000. But in those moments when I am true to myself, it really comes down to this one compact essence: I want my river back.

Freedom's just another million words

Edmonton, Alberta, March 1996

April will bring a remarkable change in my life. For the first time, I will be able to write with confidence in my mother tongue. I have always been able to speak Oriya, and read it on a printed page. But I cannot write without embarrassing myself. When my family came to Canada, I brought with me the Oriya I learned to write as a child—large, clumsy characters, with none of the easy grace that comes with written fluency.

Come April, I will be able to acquire, for $24.95 U.S., a Macintosh Oriya font. Once it's paid for, I can bring it right into my computer, thanks to the Internet. If it weren't for this worldwide network that enables computers to talk to one anther, I might never have found out an Oriya font is being developed.

For the first time, I'll be able to write to uncles and aunts and cousins in the language they know best. I can even contribute to the store of writing in one of the world's small languages—one with only thirty-two million native speakers. I cannot properly explain the sense of wonder I feel.

My elation is tempered by the fundamental concerns others raise. The Internet is also a repository of evil. Pedophilia, terrorism, acts of subversion, are all to be found in the information anyone may post for others to read. It is in effect the largest bulletin board in the world, open to all comers, with no discrimination between the worthwhile and the scurrilous, with no moral guidepost, no control. Punch in any politician's name, and you will get articles full of terrible and slanderous things no newspaper would dare to print. If you want a conspiracy theory, you will find one to match every taste.

If we act prudently, reasonably, honourably, there is no need to fear what the Internet offers. The problem, of course, is many humans don't act that way—or at least, not all the time. The question it raises is this: are we ready or able to handle real freedom? The Internet becomes like life itself. There are good choices and poor choices, and there are consequences to each. As with so many technological advances, it is not the technology itself that is good or evil, but the use humans make of it. There are no limits to behaviour in this global marketplace of ideas—it is so free it could justly be called anarchy.

There is another significant aspect to the Internet. Almost all other technology is proprietary: it belongs to someone, it belongs to government, and someone or the other regulates it. The Internet is virtually impossible to regulate: you might be able to develop "gatekeepers" to prevent unsavoury material from being circulated, but someone will find a way around it as soon as the barrier goes up.

It's hopeless to ask the companies that provide Internet service to regulate the content. At Netscape, the most popular Internet browser, forty-five million uses are recorded every day—and the number is growing almost exponentially. How do you control that? All one needs is access to a computer that has a connection to communicate with others.

How on earth is a repressive government going to control this flow of information? In the dying days of the Soviet empire, the fax machine became a powerful weapon—a message could be sent to or from just about anywhere in the world. The Internet is far more pervasive. Unless the repressive country is technologically backward and determined to remain so, the spread of Internet technology can strike blows for freedom.

Part of my Internet reading includes *Kompas,* the Catholic daily published in Jakarta. Indonesia, the world's fourth most populous country, offers a classic example of an authoritarian government that is trying to keep a tight leash on politics and social agitation even as a surging economy creates a huge middle class. Indonesia's better newspapers are best read between the lines. Journalists can only go so far before they court government reprisal. In the March 1 edition, a *Kompas* story quotes a human-rights activist who supports an independent commission to monitor the next national elections. The mere existence of the monitoring body, writes *Kompas,* will raise the political awareness that is essential to building a civil society. It's a clever bit of writing, because the phrase "civil society" is in English—as though it were a foreign concept, alien to the Indonesian experience. Normally, any foreign phrase is translated into Bahasa Indonesia.

What does it mean? Not much, as one story. But over time, in the context of other stories, there's an emerging picture of a strong impetus for democracy among educated Indonesians—and the on-line edition of *Kompas* is most likely to be read by Indonesians studying or living abroad. They can send their comments and opinions directly to the newspaper—and to each other—with relatively little worry of a government interception. Or if they send a message as carefully code-worded as the *Kompas* report, the meaning will be clear enough. Governments get nervous about things beyond their control—especially information. Trying to regulate communications on the Internet is akin to catching raindrops. You'll get some, but how can you possibly get them all?

Unless someone develops the technology to permits widespread monitoring and control—a barrier that will prompt someone else to develop a bypass—the Internet is as close to utter freedom as anyone can come. No one can control your speech or expression.

No one can claim ownership of the invention, nor retain the ability to decide who may or may not use it. It is a freedom that carries an awesome responsibility—and whether we can handle it or not, it is here to stay. Philosophers and democrats have led, over the centuries, the quest for genuine human freedom. Now that it is here, in compelling and seductive form, what do we do with it?

A postscript, February 1999

The freedom conferred by the information age is the central freedom of the borderless world, the very freedom that breaks boundaries between nations, individuals, and communities. No fortress walls, no tureens of scalding oil, no barbed-wire boundaries can stop the freedom the Internet confers. The world learned of the Tiananmen Square massacres by facsimile and telephone. The power of computer-driven communications is even more pervasive. When Suharto's secret police shot students at Trisakti University in May 1998, the banned newsmagazine *Tempo*, which continued to maintain a presence on the World Wide Web, instantly put up a condolence page that drew response from across the globe. Dictators may continue to repress, the mighty may continue to exploit the weak; but someone somewhere will come to know something about it. The instinct to set boundaries, to define territories individual and collective, will not easily be lost from the human experience. Yet in this age, at the cusp of the millennium, we have the capacity to permeate all boundaries. What is to be done with it? Perhaps the answer belongs to one of the century's more perceptive poets, George Seferis. The 1963 Nobel Laureate clearly sets out the path:

> And if the soul is to know itself
> It must look into a soul:
> The stranger and enemy,
> We have seen him in the mirror.